FINESSE

SURVIVAL GUIDE

TO THE

AMERICAN LEGAL BATTLEFIELD

By MARCUS SWAN

FOUNDER OF NATURALOSOPHY

Naturalosophy Publishing LLC
Swan@naturalosophy.com

© Copyright – 2023

All Rights Reserved. No part of this book may be reproduced, stored in a retrieval system, or transmitted by any means without the author's written permission.

Printed in the United States of America

ISBN: 979-8-9890425-0-0

Editing, book cover, design, and interior formatting by Naturalosophy Publishing.

Dedication

I dedicate this book to my baby brother Darrell "Dee-Dee" Jackson, Walk Light Bay-bro; our day is coming. Patience, Focus, and Finesse will get us through!

And

To the loving memory of my little brother Eddie "Rel-Rel" Jackson. Forever my Brother's Keeper

TABLE OF CONTENTS

CONTENTS	1
PREFACE	3
1: Finesse	10
❖ Developing a Legal Mentality	
2: Habits and Habitats	19
❖ The Mechanisms of the Courtroom	
3: Weapons of War	29
❖ Constitutions and the Rights We Deprive Them	
4: Locked and Loaded	51
❖ The True Nature of Caselaw	
5: Rules of Engagement	64
❖ The Manner of Legal Engagement	
6: Allies or Adversaries	83
❖ Interacting with Attorneys	
7: A One-Man Army	93
❖ The Nuances of Self-Representation	
8: The Peace Treaty Agreement	98
❖ Approaching Plea Bargains	
9: The Best Offense is a Good Defense	119
❖ The Importance of Having a Defense	
10: Brother in Arms	128
❖ The Dynamics of Co-Defendants	
11: Classified Intel	133
❖ The Purpose of Discovery	

12: Are You Not Entertained? Isn't This Why You're Here!   145
   ❖ The Prosecutor's Trial Tactics

13: Controlling the Narrative   155
   ❖ The Importance of Establishing the Theory

14: The Stages of Battle   175
   ❖ The Legal Process

15: The Last Stand   196
   ❖ The Trial

16: The End Game   228
   ❖ The Appellate Process

Exhibits
   ❖ Attachment One   267
   ❖ Attachment Two   273
   ❖ Attachment Three   278
   ❖ Attachment Four   280
   ❖ Attachment Five   282
Notes   284

PREFACE

The intention of this book is not to provide people with a means to manipulate the legal system. Not every defendant lodged in the criminal justice system is a criminal. This book is instead a guide that I hope provides the lost caught in the clutches of the justice system with an opportunity for a second chance. I say lost because, contrary to what many believe, a defendant's charge does not always define them. Many defendants in the system would take full advantage of any ounce of compassion, using the entire process as a learning experience and incentive to live a law-abiding life. Unfortunately, this does not happen in most cases, resulting in these individuals languishing in prisons far longer than justice should require. For the many defendants with no financial means to defend themselves and charged with crimes providing no hope of a future if convicted, a second chance looks a lot different than it would for individuals coming into the system with minor charges that naturally afford them multiple chances anyway. In a sense, I'm saying that defendants with more severe charges are afforded less leniency than defendants with less severe charges, which sounds sensible, right? However, a large grey area exists because our criminal justice system is far more business-oriented than justice-oriented. The mercy and compassion alluded to earlier can be extended to any defendant for any charge, no matter how egregious the crime, just if one can financially play the game. Moreover, playing the game entails nothing more than paying an expensive attorney to either A) Broker you a favorable plea, B) Find a legal loophole to dispose of the case or C) Get you a mistrial or acquitted of the charges altogether. Thus, this means a second chance is possible under the right circumstances for defendants with serious charges but no means to hire an expensive attorney. However, that second chance is only possible if one can finesse the legal process to allow you to leverage your plea, find your loophole, or precipitate your acquittal or mistrial, which brings me to the purpose of this book, which is to aid defendants in securing a second chance utilizing understanding how this process works in a way to exploit it. In the same way, for individuals whose expensive attorneys can get them acquitted or get cases thrown out because of loopholes and secure favorable plea bargains, there are steps you can take to bring about the same results. If society and the criminal justice system will not afford you the second chance you need, you must at least try to create your second chance.

This book is also inspired to serve as a warning of how vindictive, biased, and hypocritical the criminal justice system truly is in America. As statistics show, minorities from low-income and crime-infested backgrounds and those whose parents have been to prison stand a much higher chance of also going to prison. If reading this book gives you a bleak impression of the hopelessness in this system for many defendants, it just may serve as a prison-saving deterrent.

The unadulterated freedom we enjoy in our society as Americans naturally encourages the younger generation to live on the edge, take chances, and push the limits. And it seems with each generation, the youth is becoming increasingly delusional about the consequences of those risks. It is not until their delusion dissipates because of some limit they cross that they realize the actual reality and gravity of what they have done. Yet, this plays out very differently depending on your social status. On the one hand, you have the youth from privileged backgrounds whose circumstances and environment bring about risk-taking in the form of drunk driving, experimenting with drugs, fighting, running away from home, destruction of private property, petty theft, and crimes of this nature. It is not due to some moral superior predisposition that their crimes come off as petty mischief. Their social circumstances are what prevent the necessity of such grave risks. On the other hand, you have the youth from disadvantaged backgrounds whose circumstances facilitate risk-taking, which often comes in the form of murder, robbery, battery, grand larceny, prostitution, and drug dealing. The instability of their social circumstances is the cause of their risk-taking being much more dangerous and offensive than their counterparts. To the desensitized youth from underprivileged backgrounds, such risks are expected and seen as no less severe than the risks the privileged youth are susceptible to in their environments.

With enough objectivity, it is easy to see this as a matter of one being a product of one's environment. However, this does not render the underprivileged youth any less capable of correction than the privileged youth, regardless of the difference in nature of such crimes.

By now, you may be wondering how any of this is relative. This is relative because when these two groups are ultimately prosecuted in the criminal justice system for these risks/crimes, one group can use the experience to wake up from their illusion, correct their behavior, and move forward to live productive lives. While they lawfully prosecute the other group to such an extent that even if they awaken from their illusion and learn their lesson, they are left unable to recover from the situation because of harsh sentences. This is truly what it means to be a victim of circumstance here in America. This is all relative because I once was one of the many youths from an underprivileged background who committed many of these same risks. Which is why, to this day, I have a substantial prison sentence hanging over my head. For this reason, defendants must acquaint themselves with the true nature of the criminal justice system as laid out in this book.

Because again, the only second chance you may have in the end is the one you create for yourself.

Innocent until proven guilty is the idea they impress upon you when you catch a case, but do you feel innocent as you sit locked up in the county jail? To further reinforce this misconception, this system insists that you hire an attorney to represent you during the proceedings, even to the extent of providing you one free of charge if you cannot afford one. In court, these attorneys stand up on your behalf in such a way that makes you feel secure. They say what you cannot say, do what you cannot do, and they understand the things you do not understand. The effect of representation renders defendants like helpless children in need of protection. When fighting a case, all of these things disarm you from developing the mentality necessary for victory. This book is not a call to disregard representation altogether but to overthrow the helpless mentality many succumb to because of this system. This book is a means to provide you with the finesse to fight your case because that is exactly what a criminal prosecution is: a fight.

America has one of the largest prison populations in the world, not because everyone in America is a criminal but because the criminal justice system has become a self-sustaining entity with one underlying objective: convictions. This system does not train its police officers to maintain order but to initiate convictions. It does not train its prosecutors to represent State interests but rather to secure convictions. And it does not train judges to administer justice but rather to administer convictions. As a result, we see in real-time the exploitation of those supposedly innocent until proven guilty. In many instances, the criminal justice system is not utilizing justice to bring about guilt. This system is taking advantage of those ignorant of the law to bring about their convictions.

1

"FINESSE"

Developing a Legal Mentality

They finally got you. You were out there recklessly, doing the most, living as if no consequences were coming behind your actions. Nevertheless, I want you to understand I get it. If nobody gets it, I get it. I have been in the same situation you're in right now. I have been in the county jail with charges that would have the average person thinking I might never return to the streets. I battled with the same thoughts going through your head right now. Thoughts like, I must be dumb to be in this situation. However, for this book, you should understand that your circumstances are not necessarily a product of your stupidity. And even if you are stupid, you cannot always presume that is why you caught your case. You could have the most careless individual in the world do the same thing you did, and they may never have gotten caught. You're getting caught only equates to one simple truth: your luck finally ran out. In the same breath, I also tell you that you should have foreseen this coming from a mile away. A life of breaking the law involves luck, chance, and risk. You do not have to be a mathematician to understand that dealing with probabilities is always hit-and-miss. You should have anticipated that eventually, your luck would run out. I can hear you now, "Well, my situation is different, "but at this point, none of that even matters. The fact that you are in this situation right now makes any other factor obsolete. It doesn't matter that you made every effort to dot all your I's and cross all your T's, and it doesn't matter that you planned everything out to the end. None of this means anything when, despite all of that, some unforeseen circumstance sealed your fate. Therefore, I am telling you that it is all about the numbers when you break the law. And as the saying goes: "Men lie, women lie, numbers don't."

From an analytical perspective, the numbers tell us that the odds of catching a case are infinite for those in the business of breaking the law. This means, on the one hand, there are an infinite number of ways to catch a case, but on the other hand, there is no surefire way of guaranteeing never to be caught other than not taking the chance at all. To explain this, look at breaking the law as a video game. Video games do not create themselves but are products of human ingenuity. The creators of these games are the architects who created the foundation for beating the game as well as losing the game. Anytime you talk about beating any video game, what you are referring to is the predesigned set of moves, choices, or configurations that programmers design to bring about the victory of that game. However, the problem with the game we play is that no predetermined configuration is designed for winning.

This means there is not one specific set of moves that guarantees victory in this game. The game of breaking the law is unnatural, causing its outcomes to be probabilistic, uncertain, and unreliable. This is not to say that everybody who plays this game goes to jail, as certain individuals manage to slip through the cracks, like winning the Powerball lottery. While countless people play, only a tiny percentage of individuals win. If you play long enough, eventually, you will lose.

Please do not get it twisted. The intention behind this book is not to try to convince you to change your ways. Nope, it's not something I am trying to accomplish because what you are doing with your life is your prerogative. It would be best if you did what you think is best for you and your family, the same way I must do what's best for me and my family. Nevertheless, it's essential to understand the numbers behind this situation, as you have likely become accustomed to living on blind chance and delusion.

Like right now, you're probably sitting in the county jail facing all this time but feeding yourself false hope to keep your composure. You're probably not even worried about the situation. The gravity of the situation probably hasn't even hit you yet. You're probably telling yourself it'll all work out, or you're good because that's what the people around you are telling you. You have probably been in a similar situation in the past and received a slap on the wrist, reassuring you that this time will be the same. These are mere defense mechanisms we use to cope with our reality. The fact of the matter is this could be the beginning of the end for you. The time you spend in jail during the pretrial stages of your case may be your best hope of saving yourself. But before you take this situation seriously, you must put things in the proper perspective. This starts by letting go of all delusion and false hope because, in this situation, neither hope nor delusion will do you any good. At this point, relying on luck or some other stroke of good fortune is legal suicide.

To develop **finesse**,[1] **you first must** get rid of the idea of a guaranteed future with whatever significant other you had in your life before you caught this case. The first year of fighting a severe case is always one of the most crucial. Rather than trying to understand what is truly at stake, most people squander this crucial period trying to preserve, maintain, and cultivate stronger ties with their significant other, which is only a defensive mechanism to indulge one's hope. Trying to hold on to your significant other while fighting a case is hope-oriented and delusional. If this individual were your main priority, there would be no need or urgency to solidify ties at such a crucial time. If this individual were who you believe them to be, such ties would already be secure. This is probably the worst possible time to try to solidify such ties because if you have scorned your significant other, they will undoubtedly utilize this time to make you pay for how you mistreated them in the past. Furthermore, it is essential to understand that most women in these situations physically move on after roughly 2-3 months anyway. You must realize the most important thing to do is tend to your situation, your freedom, and your future. Suppose you genuinely love and want a relationship with this individual. In that case, the only way to make this a reality is by disposing of the case against you as soon as possible; otherwise, you might as well let it go, and it's always psychologically better you initiate this separation rather than vice versa.

The next idea you need to let go of is one that your friends and family will support you throughout this fight. At the beginning of your case, you may receive all of the support in the world, but as months go by, what tends to happen is all of that support gradually fades. I am telling you that it would be wild not to accept whatever assistance or support you receive graciously, but don't expect it in this situation. Because to expect and not receive creates a bitterness that interferes with one's focus throughout this process. This situation will teach you how most people only love you for the immediate purpose you serve them. And the sooner you cease to provide that purpose, the sooner the love dissipates.

The next idea to beware of during this process is the idea that you're going to find some significant flaw in the case that leads to you having the whole case dismissed just like that. Please do not allow this idea to dominate your focus because it will mislead and distract you. This is not to imply that this never happens. Yes, there are some instances where Courts dismiss cases, but this does not happen often.

This usually happens when there is a structural error, a jurisdictional issue, or a complete lack of evidence. But make no mistake, a Judge rarely dismisses a violent or severe charge before trial on a mere technicality. Most courts would rather risk convicting you and having you win your appeal by technicality rather than dismissing the case before trial. This mentality of wanting a case dismissed before trial can sometimes weaken your fighting spirit and blind you to the bigger picture. In this situation, the bigger picture is that a win comes in many different forms. Sometimes, a win can be you getting 15 years for a murder charge that carries a life sentence. A win could be you getting 10 years for a drug charge that holds 20 years. A win in this situation is anything you can recover from and afterward live somewhat of a full life. This is not some game of seeking and finding where a glitch you come across wins you the game. Any legal battle is war; victory comes only through will, tactics, execution, and most importantly, patience. Make sure to prepare yourself accordingly.

This brings me to the last idea and the overall theme of this book, which is we must approach this situation for the fight that it truly is. Not only is it a fight.

This is a war. The stakes are just as high as any real war because losing this fight could result in you losing your legal and physical life. And anybody who approaches this process as anything less is asking for disaster. This is a fight you cannot afford to be naive about. You cannot shy away or avoid it. But most importantly, this is a fight you cannot lose without putting forth an effort. There are a lot of people who sit in jail wasting their time, not realizing that they should be using this crucial time as a means of gaining an advantage.

2

"HABITS AND HABITATS"

The Mechanism of the Courtroom

Once you have done away with the false ideas distorting your reality, only then are you ready to understand the true gravity of this situation. The first point of emphasis in any war is analyzing and exploiting the habits and habitats of your adversary. As you familiarize yourself with this information beforehand, this provides you with an adversarial advantage. Acquiring an understanding of the habits and habitats of your adversary could very well be the determining factor leading to victory or defeat.

In this situation, the habit and habitat of your adversary is multi-faceted. It begins first by understanding the habitat, which is the Courtroom. When most people walk into a courtroom and see the aura of judges as they sit elevated above the rest of the room like some god on judgment day, this often leads to a mistaken presumption that your enemy is the judge, but this is erroneous thinking.

> "The role of a trial judge in a criminal case is not merely that of an observer or even that of referee enforcing the rules of the game (See People v. De Jesus.). In fulfillment of its broader obligation to ensure the defendant a fair and impartial trial (People v. Crimmins), a Court is not without power, to be exercised with judicious restraint, to keep the proceedings within the reasonable confines of the issues and to encourage clarity rather than obscurity in the development of proof (See People v. Knapper.)"

What this means is the Judge, in your case is nothing more than an overseer of this battle rather than your enemy. The caselaw above would even convey that Judges serve more of a purpose to you than the prosecutor. Unfortunately, things are not as black and white as the law makes them, so oftentimes, Judges will be more partial to your adversary, especially if you happen to be a lower-class minority. The most effective way to prompt judges to embody this intended role as impartial overseers is by directly or indirectly engaging the court in a way that demonstrates that you have some form of legal competence. How you should go about doing this is explained in later chapters.

Now that we have established that the Judge is not your adversary, it is time to identify the real enemy, which requires an analogy. This process of catching a case and having your freedom legally voided is comparable to having your personhood transformed into a legal instrument known as a title. A title is no diferent from any other title one acquires to claim ownership of a certain property you purchase. The Black's Law Dictionary (9th edition) defines Title as *the union of all elements (as ownership, possession, and custody) constituting the legal right to control and dispose of property; the legal link between a person who owns property and property itself.* By now, you might be thinking, "Title? I am not some document; I may be incarcerated but I'm still a human being." And my response to that is while you may not be a title per se, the legal instrument indicating that you are now indebted to the State is called an indictment. And suppose you're convicted and committed to the department of corrections. In that case, this indictment will then be converted into a final judgment, which functions very much like a title by way of being transferable from one owner to another. The criminal justice system demonstrates this by transferring a defendant's indictment or final judgment from one jurisdiction to another or from a misdemeanor Court to a felony court. For example, when you go to jail, your case begins initially in the lower court that only oversees misdemeanor and traffic offenses. If your charges do not fit into this category, the lower Court will transfer your case to a higher Court designated for more serious felonies. This transfer process occurs through a Grand Jury Hearing. At this hearing, a group of jurors will determine if there is enough probable cause to issue an indictment and transfer your case to felony court. If this happens, at that point the criminal justice system considers your personhood nothing more than an indictment that is suspended in legal litigation. This whole process is very similar to a custody hearing! This means that until your case is resolved you belong neither to yourself nor to the State. You are now in essence a title. And the entity competing for ownership of your title is none other than the State in which you are being charged. Obviously, the State is not a real person and cannot physically defend its own interest. It is the prosecuting attorney that represents and embodies the state's interest. And this is who your real opponent is in this battle. This is the only true adversary you have in this war.

In most sports, there is always a team on offense and a team on defense. Victory in any sport is a matter of formulating the best offensive strategy that counteracts the opposition's defense and vice versa. This same principle applies in legal battles as well. The key to attaining victory in any battle is by first identifying and understanding when it's best to take a position of offense and when you should be in a position of defense. Understanding this key factor further enables you to exploit and weaken your adversary's power. The ignorance of this has led to the squandering of many possible victories in court. The criminal justice system is structured in such a way that it can lead people astray right from the beginning. A prime example of this is the assignment of the term 'Defendant' to those who are accused. By branding someone with this label, it implies a necessity to adopt a defensive posture in legal proceedings. This label can create a false impression that winning the case is only possible by taking a defensive stance rather than proving one's theory. Or in other words, passively sitting back and figuratively baiting the prosecution to give you their best shot, rather than engaging in the battle. The logic behind the concept of being 'defendants' derives from prosecutors having the burden of proof[2] in this process. Which means in criminal cases, the prosecutor has the 'burden' of proving you are guilty, and that the onus is not on you to prove your innocence. But the idea of a burden of proof is a vicious trap, so take heed before taking it at face value. I say this because the idea of a burden of proof conveys the impression that the jury will automatically assume your innocence during trial, something that is false, false, and false. Keep in mind, the question of your guilt hinges on the belief of everyday people and everyday people will not give anybody the benefit of doubt but will always expect both parties to present their truth. This burden of proof has misled 'defendants' into believing that they need not argue their truth, challenge, or prove their innocence, which is a fatal mistake. You would be foolish not to take up this burden of proving your own innocence or proving the insufficiency of the evidence against you, just as aggressively as the prosecution will be attempting to prove your guilt.

In this book, I will provide various concepts I have constructed l call 'legal ideates' which are meant to provide you with a clear idea of certain legal concepts relative to this process. I am presenting these ideas only as a means of clarification. They are meant only to broaden your perspective and should not be confused as binding legal authority one can cite in Court. The first of these legal ideates is what I call **the 'defendant's mentality**[3] which correlates with what I have mentioned prior about not falling for the concept of a burden of proof. To have a defendant's mentality is to essentially hand yourself over on a silver platter by believing that the burden of proof is not on you to meet. Throughout your case, you must remember that you're simultaneously on both offense and defense in a criminal case. There are times to be on the offensive, and there are times to be on the defensive and this is how you should approach the entire pre-trial phase of your case. Because during the pretrial stage of the case, everything the prosecution does is for the purpose of setting the 'structural' stage for trial. Most defendants lose trials not because the evidence is so overwhelming against them, but because the prosecution manages to exploit a key piece of evidence during pretrial that ultimately becomes a major factor during the trial. In this phase of the case, prosecutors will strategically manipulate and exploit the facts of the case, the evidence, and the court rules to increase their chances of winning. Therefore, you should make sure to equip yourself with a mentality that will enable you to anticipate and counteract every move, motion, and objection the prosecution makes during this phase of the case. During this, you must also strive not to lose sight of your ultimate strategy and remember to utilize the pretrial phase as a means of setting the stage for your power move during trial. One of the main purposes of pretrial is to establish which evidence is admissible and inadmissible in a way that complements your defense.

What it all boils down to is the mentality you employ in your approach to this war. The wrong mentality will equip you with the wrong ideas, as many of the ideas we presume to be fundamental to the legal process are not what they seem. The idea that you have a right to remain silent, that you are innocent until proven guilty, and that your decision not to testify on your own behalf cannot be held against you, all can be misleading in certain respects. Concerning your right to remain silent, you should never say something to incriminate yourself but there are in fact certain instances during this process where remaining silent might cost you. In terms of being innocent until proven guilty, you would have to be naive to believe the notion that the judge, the prosecution or a jury is approaching this process as if you are truly innocent. In terms of testifying on your own behalf, even if the law dictates that your decision not to testify on your own behalf is not to be a factor of guilt, no judge can change a juror's opinion that innocent people will always testify on their own behalf. There have been many situations where a defendant's failure to testify on their own behalf was likely the determining factor in them losing their case. Therefore, it is best not to go into this war with a black and white approach because what you will realize is that there is a lot of grey areas.

3

"WEAPONS OF WAR"

Constitutions and the Right to Deprive Them

In any war, there can be no hope of victory without one resource: weapons. You need weapons for your defense, and you need weapons for your attack. In this war, the United States Constitution along with your respective State Constitution will provide you your most formidable weapons, which are the five Amendments relative to all criminal cases.

Your first and most vital weapons stem from your respective State Constitution. Throughout this process, it is important for you to keep in mind that if you are not fighting federal charges then your charges are alleging a violation of state criminal code, which means you are subject to the State's constitution first. This is why the indictment holding you will always emphasize two key factors: the jurisdiction where you committed the alleged offense and which state code or statute you violated. Without this information, the indictment is constitutionally insufficient. It is important that you always keep in mind that this process is a **State proceeding** that functions through State law. (Unless of course you are under a federal jurisdiction) Due to this being a state proceeding, your priority of focus should always be your State Constitution and all of the rights afforded to you under it. Which might sound like I am diminishing the power of the almighty Federal Constitution, but this is not the case. The fact of the matter is the Federal Constitution is what provides each State with the basic legal parameters of how it must lawfully prosecute its citizens. Therefore, in terms of due process, nothing in the state constitution can ever conflict with what is afforded in the Federal constitution.

This means that while prosecuting you, if the State shall ever violate your Federal rights, you have an avenue of seeking relief through the Federal courts on appeal. Nevertheless, during the trial, this leaves you wholly in the hands of your respective State constitution for protection.

To make sure that your federal rights are being respected, all 50 States have tailored their respective constitution to mimic the Federal constitution. All of the due process rights you have under your state constitution echo those you have under the Federal Constitution. The only difference is in some States you may also have additional rights the Federal Constitution does not protect. Becoming familiar with your rights under the State Constitution is an absolute must. After becoming familiar with your state constitution, your second priority is familiarizing yourself with the Federal constitution. Though I've made this a second priority, your federal rights are no less vital. I only refer to the Federal Constitution being second priority because any relief for Federal violations comes after the culmination of your state case. In essence, the Federal Constitution is what gives everything its power. It is the Federal Constitution, which is responsible for everything, from delegating authority and power to various branches of our government, to outlining the processes of electing political leaders, and providing constitutional provisions all 50 states are obliged to follow. In the context of the criminal justice system, what makes the Federal constitution so important for criminal defendants is the **Bill of Rights.** Particularly, the Bill of Rights is what provides defendants the only firepower in which to defend oneself, which I call the "5 Felony Weaponry" [4] In this war, your five Felony Weaponry are the means through which to protect oneself which are:

(1.) The Fourth Amendment which entails that, "people have a right to be secure in their persons, houses, papers and effects against unreasonable search and seizures, and shall not be violated, and no warrants shall issue, but upon probable cause, supported by Oath or affirmation. and particularly describing the place to be searched, and the persons or things to be seized."

(2.) The Fifth Amendment which entails that, "No persons shall be held to answer for a capital, or otherwise infamous crime, unless on a presentment or indictment of a Grand Jury, except in cases arising in the land or naval forces, or in the Militia, when in actual service in time of war or public danger; nor shall any person be subject for the same offense to be twice put in jeopardy of life or limb; nor shall be compelled in any criminal case to be a witness against himself, nor be deprived of life, liberty, or property, without due process of law; nor shall private property be taken for public use, without just compensation.

(3.) <u>The Sixth Amendment</u> which entails that, "in all criminal prosecutions, the accused shall enjoy a right to a speedy and public trial, by an impartial jury of the State and district where the crime shall have been committed, which district shall have been previously ascertained by law, and to be informed of the nature and cause of the accusation; to be confronted with the witness against him; to have compulsory process for obtaining witnesses in his favor, and to have the assistance of Counsel for his defense.

(4.) <u>The Eight Amendment</u> which stipulates that, "Excessive bail shall not be required, nor excessive fines imposed, nor cruel and unusual punishment inflicted."

(5.) <u>The Fourteenth Amendment</u> which stipulates that "No state shall make or enforce any law which shall abridge the privileges or immunities of citizens of the United States; nor shall any State deprive any person of life, liberty, or property, without due process of law; nor deny to any person within its jurisdiction the equal protection of the laws."

As one goes about the process of resisting the attack of the State, these five Constitutional Amendments are the means to ensure that this lopsided fight is somewhat fair. During this battle, do not just automatically expect judges, prosecutors and sometimes even attorneys to preserve, invoke or guard any of these protections for you. These Amendments are comparable to gravity, as gravity does not act upon itself but rather reacts. Though these Amendments frame the criminal justice system, you still must be diligent in making sure that your rights are respected throughout this process. It is even one of the more common strategies of prosecutors to get defendants to surrender these rights by procedurally waiving them. If at any point during this process you neglect to invoke many of the rights afforded to you, the court will most likely determine that to be an abandonment on your part of that right. You see this **with Miranda warnings** [5], which are when law enforcement officers tell defendants:

> *"You have the right to remain silent, anything you say can and will be used against you in the court of law. You have a right to an attorney, if you cannot afford one, one will be provided to you."*

Even after officers read these rights, defendants could abandon their right to remain silent by subsequently speaking in ways that are incriminating. Many of the defendants that come into the criminal justice system at a young age do not realize that this system was made with adults in mind, so when those of younger ages commit certain crimes, there is no compassion and sympathy regardless of age. When certain crimes are committed, the only compassion you will receive in a court of law is the compassion the Constitution affords you and most of the due process rights you have under the constitution comes by way of those you actively demand. Therefore, the beginning of becoming finesse begins with familiarizing yourself these five Amendments of the United States Constitution. There will always be both a State and Federal 5 Felony Weaponry at your disposal. Your fight begins by knowing what rights you are entitled to under your State Constitution as a citizen. The more fully you understand what rights you're entitled to, the more aggressive you can be in this war.

The first of these weapons is the Fourth Amendment. The Fourth Amendment requires "a *factual showing sufficient to comprise 'probable cause"* before one's person can be physically seized." Without the protection of this Fourth Amendment, Officers could randomly seize any individual and execute searches of their persons and possessions at any given time. This is exactly what police do in poor communities. However, in a perfect world, the Fourth Amendment is supposed to serve as a safeguard to protect citizens from "intrusive governmental conduct". As a free citizen of the United States, you have a fundamental right that prohibits the State from seizing you or your property without a somewhat credible reason. Which means, before police officers can physically detain you or physically search your person or possessions, there must be some factual proof that you committed a specific crime against the State. And even then, officers are subject to a designated process of detaining you in such a way that does not violate this fourth Amendment. Any arrests that are unduly aggressive or sexually invasive will violate the Fourth Amendment, leaving Officers subject to criminal liability and civil liabilities. More than anything, the Fourth Amendment serves to protect one of the things we all cherish most, our property. This Amendment is so fundamental to the values of America that even if officers were to search and obtain something illegal on your possession, if your Fourth Amendment right is violated in the process, the whole search becomes void and anything taken as a result will be rendered tainted and even sometimes returned to you, particularly money or property. The Fourth Amendment could easily be a favorite among hustlers because it constitutionally ensures you the privacy to do what may be unlawful, at least until officers can prove it through some evidence. This right is what created the necessity of arrest warrants, search warrants and probable cause hearings.

Due to the Fourth Amendment's protection from seizure of your person or property absent probable cause, search warrant affidavits must describe specifically what that probable cause entails before a judge will issue a warrant. Amid prosecutors attempting to acquire your personhood, if any of your fourth amendment rights are violated, you should immediately exercise these rights by pursuing the proper legal avenues provided under your state law. For example, if police unlawfully search your car and stumble upon a gun, you will file a motion to the court seeking to suppress that evidence because your right to unlawful Search and Seizure was violated under whatever section of your State Constitution as well as the Fourth Amendment of the United States Constitution. This Fourth Amendment may seem to apply only to incidents occurring before the proceedings, but to a lesser degree, many of these rights also extend with you into the custody of the Department of Corrections. However, when you seek relief from Fourth Amendment violations occurring in custody, they will have no bearing on the criminal case you are fighting. These types of violations are subject to civil litigation requiring the filing of a civil lawsuit.

The second weapon is the Fifth Amendment. The Fifth Amendment is probably the most popular of all of the Amendments due to it being the source of the famous expression, "I plead the fifth!" In my opinion, the Fifth Amendment is the essence of judicial self-protection. One of the rights this Amendment provides is no defendant can be compelled to offer evidence against themselves in a criminal prosecution. Its evolution has brought about other protections such as your choice not to testify on your own behalf that cannot used against you in trial and the right of protection against double jeopardy prohibiting the State from prosecuting you twice for the same offense. The Fifth Amendment is an additional due process clause protecting defendants in criminal proceedings. The violations that arise from this amendment will typically occur during both the pre-trial and trial phase. The defensive nature of the Fifth Amendment will always help you to ward off overaggressive prosecutors during the trial.

The third weapon of the defendant is the Sixth

Amendment. The Sixth Amendment serves as the "Confrontation Clause" because it provides you with a legal platform and basis to confront your accuser in various capacities. The inspiration behind the confrontation clause is originally from the beheading of someone by the name of Walter Raleigh of England whose trial and conviction rested on nothing more but one-sided affidavits from accusers. In the last letter to his wife before his death, Raleigh's words were *"That Almighty God ...teach me to forgive my persecutors and false accusers and send us to meet in his glorious Kingdom."* To ensure such meetings could take place in this life, the founders of the Constitution added this "confrontation clause" so it would require more than just accusatory affidavits to convict one of criminal charges. For what it's worth, the Sixth Amendment paved the way to the right of a trial by jury, presumption of innocence, the State's burden of proof and many of the other legal facets we see at work in the criminal justice system here in America. Consequently, this weapon is specifically significant for those planning on going to trial. One's attorney, the judge, the prosecutor, and the structural proceedings of the trial can bring about violations of the Sixth Amendment in many ways. The Sixth Amendment is versatile by way of being a means of securing your defense, attacking the prosecution's case as well as halting the prosecutions advances on your defense. One of the more potent rights to derive from the Sixth Amendment is the right to a Fast and Speedy Trial. Anytime a defendant files a Motion to the Court or orally expresses on the record their right to a fast and speedy trial under the Sixth Amendment of the United States Constitution, what this does is places the burden on the Court and the prosecutor to bring you to trial within a reasonable time. However, this right to a speedy trial has two components that many people oftentimes confuse. The first component applies to the I.A.D. (Interstate Agreement on Detainers). Section 18 USCS, Article III of the United States Constitution provides an agreement also endorsed by all of the party States that are signatories to this agreement. There are a few States that are not subject to this agreement, so one should inquire into if your respective State is under this agreement. This agreement under 18 USCS, Article 111 holds that:

> "Whenever a person has entered upon a term of imprisonment in a penal or correctional institution of a party state, and whenever during the continuance of the term of imprisonment there is pending in any other party state any untried indictment, information, or complaint on the basis of which a detainer has been lodged against the prisoner. He shall be brought to trial within one hundred and eighty days after he shall have caused to be to be delivered to the prosecuting officer and the appropriate court of the prosecutor's officer's jurisdiction written notice of the place of his imprisonment and his request for a final disposition to be made of the indictment, information, or complaint:"....

This means that if you are serving time in any of these states, and you have a pending felony in another state that is also a party to this I.A.D. agreement, you can file this I.A.D. to prompt the prosecutor in that state to try you within 180 days. If that state fails to bring you to trial within 180 days, the law requires that the charges against you shall be dismissed with prejudice[6].

However, there are certain exceptions to this agreement through which courts and prosecutors can exceed this 180-day deadline but for the most part, if this deadline is breached there is a chance to have your charges dismissed. The second component of a defendant's right to speedy trial does not involve detainers. When a defendant invokes the right to a speedy trial either on the record or by motion, the court and prosecutor has the burden of bringing the defendant to trial within a reasonable time. This second component applies to charges that are pending in the trial court and the difference is that there is no 180-day deadline such as with the I.A.D. In <u>United States v. Doggett,</u> 505, U.S. 652, the United States Supreme Court established that the violation of a Sixth Amendment request for a speedy trial applies *"as it approaches a year"*. Like the I.A.D agreement, there are also a handful of exceptions that provide the state with the luxury of also exceeding this deadline.

The Fourth weapon, which is the Eighth Amendment, traces its roots back to England's "Glorious

Revolution" of 1688-89. This revolution gave rise to England's Bill of Rights, which prohibited excessive bail, excessive fines, and cruel and unusual punishment. Out of all of the five weapons provided to defendants, this is undoubtedly the least effective in attacking or warding off the prosecutor in the pre-trial phase of the case as there is essentially no one leading caselaw to argue against an excessive bail. And if your sentence is within the parameters of the State's penal code, the appellate courts will never, no matter how excessive the sentence, provide you with relief on the grounds of cruel and unusual punishment. This amendment will mostly benefit State inmates arguing excessive force by prison officials in civil suits.

The Fifth weapon of the defendant is the Fourteenth Amendment. As it stands, the Fourteenth Amendment is what guarantees you your due process rights. The Fourteenth Amendment does not actually afford you any actual right but rather serves as a protective safeguard to ensure all States provide their citizens with the same due process and equal protection rights required by the Federal Constitution. Therefore, when constitutional violations occur, one should always invoke the Fourteenth Amendment along with any other amendment violated as a matter of formality. The Fourteenth Amendment should particularly resonate with African Americans, as one of the theories attributed to the enactment of 14th Amendment was to protect African Americans during post slavery. Bryan H. Wildenthal wrote about this theory in his legal article, 'The Fourteenth Amendment and The Bill of Rights':

> *"The dominant purpose of the Amendment, according to this 'Equal Rights Only" theory, was simply to ensure some measure of basic fairness and civil equality for the blacks then recently freed from slavery-and, more generally, for all Americans of Republican or Unionist sympathies (whether White of Black or any other race) threatened by mistreatment in the former slave states...... Whatever basic civil rights and liberties a state happened to afford lo its white inhabitants generally, it was now required to afford to blacks as well-and to all people, of*

whatever race, regardless of Republican or Unionists sympathies."

The importance of this Amendment is demonstrated by the Federal Courts holding that "the Due Process Clause of the Fourteenth Amendment must be respected, no matter how heinous the crime in question and no matter how guilty an accused may ultimately be found to be after guilt has been established in accordance with the procedure demanded by the Constitution."

As mentioned earlier, all five of these felony weaponries <u>originate</u> from the Federal constitution but are also found in your respective State constitution. Furthermore, what makes these five Amendments valuable even to this day is that their shelf life is unlimited. This means there is an infinite number of ways a prosecutor can violate one of these Amendments, so in essence they are the gift that keeps on giving. Many defendants assume when arguing constitutional violations, they are limited to a fixed set of violations predetermined beforehand. When in truth, Constitutional Amendments are but the guiding principles from which rights originate. Depending on the circumstances, new rights can always evolve from an infinite number of situations in a case. Many of the rights we now have came about on a gradual case-by-case basis. This means, there is an infinite number of ways these Amendments can be violated other than just from the situations described in caselaw.

For example, the 8th Amendment that prohibits Cruel and Unusual Punishment has given rise to many additional protections such as an inmate's right to a civilized degree of life's necessities while serving their prison sentence. Another example is the Sixth Amendment confrontation clause. The right to confront our accusers has further brought about protections such as the right to any evidence favorable to your defense. The State may have in its possession. These are just two small examples of the countless ways these five weapons afford us a multitude of rights. This multitude includes rights such as: the right to have evidence tested, and the right to have notice of charges, the right to be heard, the right to a hearing, the right to counsel, the right to self-representation, the right to remain silent, the right against self-- incrimination, the right to a fair trial, the right to appeal, the right to present a defense, the right to an accurate and complete record, the right to call witnesses, the right to jury trial, the right to a fast and speedy trial, the right to cross examine witnesses, the right to the presumption of innocence, the right to testify on your own behalf, the right not to be found guilty unless by proof beyond a reasonable doubt, right not to be tried by a judge who has an interest in the outcome.

All of these rights afford defendants a means of protection against the State, but you must exercise these weapons competently for them to be effective. The criminal justice system further dictates that defendants must argue a particular claim under the appropriate constitutional Amendment before any relief can be granted. For example, in <u>Albright v. Oliver,</u> 510 U.S. 266, a Petitioner, Albright, argued in a 1983 civil action suit that an Officer's seizure of his person deprived him of a Fourteenth Amendment due process right to be free from criminal prosecution without a finding of probable cause. The Appellate Court refused to consider the merits of

Albright's argument solely because he improperly presented his claim under the Fourteenth Amendment rather than the Fourth Amendment. Albright confused the 14th Amendment, which protects his due process rights to a fair trial, with the 4th Amendment which protects his right against unlawful search and seizure without probable cause. Albright should have argued that his civil rights were violated under both the Fourth Amendment and the 14th Amendment. This demonstrates that when you are invoking these rights, whether in a motion or an oral argument, it is imperative you understand the Constitutional Amendment protecting which right you are exercising. Not only must you understand it, but you must also include it in your argument, otherwise Courts will not provide you relief. As petty as this seems, this is the way it is. Appellate courts will give little to no consideration as to how the State argues against you and will never nitpick the arguments of the prosecution but will always hold the defendant to the highest and most stringent standard possible. To avoid such mishaps, you must always remember the Due Process Clause protected under the

5th and 14th Amendment is the source of all rights relative to the structural mechanisms of the trial. The 4th Amendment is the source of all of the rights relative to the State seizing and searching your person without probable cause. The 6th Amendment is the source of rights relative to confronting your accusers. And the 8th Amendment is the source of rights relative to you being excessively punished.

So again, as the State attempts to acquire legal ownership of your indictment, you can defend against their attacks by invoking these Amendments for protection. In fact, one could invoke these amendments if you believe something may even potentially infringe on one of these rights throughout the trial. With creativity, you should foresee and anticipate how a matter, or a Courts ruling could somehow infringe on these rights. These five felony weaponries may serve as your only means of survival in this process. For defendants facing felony offenses, it's imperative you make sure you have fully familiarized yourself with the Federal and State Constitution, which manufactures all of the rights you have been guaranteed.

4

"LOCKED AND LOADED"

The True Nature of the Caselaw

During war, you can have all of the weapons in the world, but they mean nothing without the ammunition necessary to exercise them. The adversary you're at war with will not flinch in the face of you merely drawing weapons with no bullets. In fact, threatening the prosecutor with unloaded weapons will only expose your unskillfulness and inability to win this war and in some cases make your adversary even more aggressive. In a legal setting, prosecutors are like wolves in that when they smell blood it only adds to their aggression in prosecuting you. Thus, it is best you accumulate as much ammunition as possible so when you draw any of these five weaponries you can exercise them effectively. In this situation, the symbolic ammunition you would use to load your 5-felony weaponry is caselaw [7]. It is almost impossible to exercise your constitutional amendments in a court of law without caselaw. The reason being is judges in the criminal justice system orientate themselves like kings. Throughout history, kings have always fabricated the impression that they possess some type of royalty, which distinguishes them from those subject to their authority. In the criminal justice system, the idea is that a judge's legal education and experience provides them with the exclusive capacity to interpret and apply the Constitution as the founders of this nation originally intended it. If you ever try to use your own personal understanding and experience as to what the Constitution dictates, the courts will intellectually reject you, no matter how valid your understanding and reasoning. For this reason, caselaw must be used when exercising these weapons against the State; otherwise, it's like shooting blanks. Caselaw are cases that have worked their way through the legal process, which afterwards proceed to the appellate courts. While in the appellate courts, a panel of judges adjudicates the claims presented on appeal, considering the arguments through the prism of their reasoning, and understanding. The ultimate assessment that they apply to the case is what in legal terms is called a "findings of fact and conclusion of law". And these 'findings of fact and conclusion of law' judges will explain how the Constitution applies to a given argument. These cases and the rulings applied to them are called caselaw, and it is the reasoning and understanding provided in these cases that one must use to exercise the 5-felony weaponry.

Another important characteristic of caselaw is that it serves as a compass for other judges to make further rulings. It is important to remember those who work for the criminal justice system are practically robots, as they are all conditioned and programed to act and think within a well- defined circuit. Therefore, your circuit court judge is not really making decisions at their own discretion. Circuit Court judges are limited to the precedent former judges and higher courts have set for them to follow. For example, in situations where you file motions to the court for pretrial release, such as with bail or supervised release, the judge's decision will normally mimic whatever precedent has been previously set. If you ever want an idea of how a judge will rule on a particular motion you want to file just look up how that judge or past judges have ruled on issues prior, or on what caselaw advises in such situations. Because typically, this is what your trial judge is going to do before making certain rulings. Caselaw will not usually address issues regarding pretrial releases but in caselaw, there will always be the 'legal ideate' I call, *Case-language.* [8] Case-language is another means of guidance through which judges make many of their decisions. For example, caselaw by way of <u>Barker v. Wingo,</u> 407 U.S., 514 conveys the following language:

"In addition, persons released on bond for lengthy periods awaiting

trial have an opportunity to commit other crimes.

It must be of little comfort to the residents of Christian County, Kentucky, lo know that Barker was at large on bail for over four years while accused of a vicious and brutal murder of which he was ultimately convicted.

Moreover, the longer an accused is free awaiting trial, the more tempting becomes his opportunity to jump bail and escape,"

The very language of this case regarding the granting of bail to defendants accused of violent crimes is one of disapproval. The tone of the language in this case resonated powerfully throughout the entire criminal justice system. In hindsight, the first thing the appellate court did in this case language was scold the trial judge for granting the defendant a reasonable bail to begin with and the second thing this language did was change the status quo for other trial judges in similar situations regarding bail. The above case was published in 1972, so one can assume up until that point, judges on the trial level were rightfully upholding constitutional ideas that 'bail should not be excessive' due to the idea that 'defendants are innocent until proven guilty.' The language in the above case, single handedly changed this sentiment not through a particular ruling but by case- language. This subtle case-language further provided trial judges a compass to use when making bail reduction rulings from that point forward.

    In essence, anytime you file a motion, you can expect your trial Court judge to parrot pre-existing caselaw. After a ruling, you may have the impression the judge has made some executive decision at his or her own discretion, when this is not the case. To save face, most circuit judges will never transparently admit this on the record, but the degree of power any judge has will always correlate with the intellectual discretion their level of court provides them. Similarly, in caselaw the inherent power of each judge is determined by the court it holds, so the higher the court, the higher the authority of the judge. I call this legal ideate the Precedential Pyramid [9].

In this pyramid, the lowest in the precedential pyramid are the judges in the District Courts or Common plea courts. These judges have authority to exercise discretion over minor cases such as those of misdemeanor, family court and traffic offenses. In such situations, there is no relative caselaw from judges on this level.

Next, in the Pyramid are the judges who occupy the Circuit or Superior courts. These Judges have the authority to exercise discretion over felony offenses. These judges are trial court judges whose authority surpasses those of District and Common Pleas judges. These judges have the limited discretion to decide pretrial releases, enforce trial court rules, and adjudicate indictment and jurisdictional matters, etc. Circuit judges will typically issue findings of fact and conclusions of law that consist only of explaining how their rulings conform to caselaw rather than establishing any kind of precedent in their own right.

Next, in the Precedential Pyramid are the judges

who occupy the State appellate courts. The difference in authority between Circuit Court judges and State appellate Court judges is Circuit judges can only uphold the constitution and precedent set out in caselaw, while State appellate judges create State caselaw and further interpret the state constitution. State appellate judges have the intellectual discretion not only to create State precedent but also issue orders the Circuit State court must follow.

Next, in the Precedential Pyramid are the judges who occupy the State Supreme Court. These judges are not merely judges but are known as Justices. The authority of the Justices who occupy the Supreme Court of the State reigns absolute on the State level. These judges have full intellectual discretion to establish or overrule state caselaw and issue orders District judges, Circuit judges and lower State appellate judges are wholly subject to uphold. These justices collectively interpret and explicate their state constitution serving as constitutional overseers of all State judges in this system.

On the State level, State Supreme Court Justices are the highest in authority, but even higher in authority than State Supreme Court Justices, are Federal Judges. Judges on the Federal level also have their own similar precedential hierarchy. When using Federal caselaw, you must first understand that each of the 50 states fall under one of the 13 Federal Judicial Circuits. For example, Kentucky, Michigan, Ohio, and Tennessee all fall under the Federal Sixth Circuit. While Connecticut, New York and Vermont all fall under the Federal Second Circuit. Therefore, after determining your State's Federal Circuit. The precedential pyramid in that Circuit is no different from the state, with Federal District courts beholden to that of the higher Circuit Courts. Though the trial court is bound to enforce caselaw from the Federal district court, many of the issues presented in these cases will not be relative to your situation. However, if you do find caselaw dealing with an issue relevant to your circumstances, you can cite these caselaws only to further validate your state arguments, but make sure to try in cite caselaw from the Federal Circuit your state falls under. The next highest on the federal precedential pyramid are judges who occupy the Federal Circuit Court of Appeals. The judges who occupy this Court have discretion to overrule any decision made in the lower federal District court. Again, your trial judge is legally bound to uphold the Federal Circuit Court of Appeals caselaw but again many of the issues on this level deal with Federal Rules of Civil Procedure, which are rules that govern the federal proceedings. However, if you were to find caselaw that could help your state arguments, do so using the caselaw from the Federal Circuit of your State.

The next and highest of all Judges on the federal precedential pyramid is United States Supreme Court. The authority of the judges who occupy this Court is universally absolute. It is the President himself that hand picks these justices. For this reason, United States Supreme Court caselaw is the law of the land and is compulsory on all judges to abide by no matter what court they occupy. But as mentioned earlier, the only issues this Court concerns itself with are the infringements of the Federal Constitution. This Court has always been notoriously careful not to interfere with decisions made in State trial courts or State appellate courts that are purely based on State law unless these decisions somehow conflict with Federal law. In a perfect judicial system, the mention of United States Supreme Court caselaw should yield considerable influence. But the sad truth is we do not live in a perfect judicial system. It just may happen that your trial judge may refuse to acknowledge any State or Federal caselaw you cite and invoke. Disheartening as it may be, this is something many judges will do. The reasoning behind this is many Circuit judges are so inexperienced and afraid to make any type of ruling that would benefit a defendant in a way that would reflect negatively on their political career, they would rather disregard the law, violate your rights, and have you appeal their decision instead. In such cases, you can only hope the appellate courts are more reasonable, something that is becoming increasingly rare in today's criminal justice system.

So again, the only way to exercise or implement the rights provided to you by your Five Felony Weaponries, is by using caselaw that supports and complements your arguments. In essence, this is almost like having to think and put together an argument with someone else's reasoning, which in this case be caselaw!

Because of this, arguing or rather litigating your claims is not as difficult as many may presume; the real obstacle for many people is in comprehending the principles a particular case may establish. As many defendants too hastily presume to comprehend what principle a caselaw is establishing, only to later realize they are mistaken. Therefore, we must understand a key is useless without a lock to put it in. In this situation, caselaw is the key that defendants must use to unlock and initiate their constitutional rights. And anytime you have a selection as extensive as caselaw is, it is not about just finding any case but rather finding the right case, because the case is the key. Without the key, there can be no opening of the door.

For those who are not familiar with how to approach caselaw, it is best to do so in the same way you would a google search. In most institutions, there should be some type of a law library with computers with the Lexus Nexus program. Lexis Nexus or other legal research engines function very much like google by way of having to use key terms to find specific cases. In my experience, if one uses specific terms relative to a specific violation, it is easier to find cases that are most optimal for your situation. For example, if I am looking for cases that support a Sixth Amendment violation regarding witness testimony. I would use terms such as "perjured testimony" or "inadmissible testimony" or "character evidence of witness" etc. A lot of creativity is necessary when coming up with the right search terms to find the perfect case. Once you find that perfect case, everything will begin to start falling in place in terms of how you must attack the prosecution's case against you.

5

"THE RULES OF ENGAGEMENT"

The Manner of Legal Engagement

In this war, the way you engage practically everything is vital and can be the difference between victory and defeat. In every battle, there are rules of engagement and ethics of how to engage in everything. There is a specific way to engage your lawyer, there is a specific way to engage the court, and there is a set way to engage the prosecutor, etc. The failure to understand and abide by these rules of engagement can cost you more than you can afford.

A specific etiquette is necessary for every facet of these proceedings. This begins first with engaging with your attorney. Many defendants approach attorneys with the wrong mentality. It is easy to just write them off as just cogs in a machine. Which may be true, but it is our attorneys that will facilitate to the judge and prosecutor the first real impression of who we are as human beings. Outside of them being your legal representative, they are also officers of the court and because of that there is a degree of ethical consideration attorneys will automatically receive from judge or prosecutors. The impression you convey to your attorney through your tone of communication and how you conduct yourself when interacting with them will also be the same impression they directly or indirectly convey to the judge and prosecutor about you. If there is a situation such as a consideration of bail or pretrial release and the judge or prosecutor are curious as to your disposition, your attorney's opinion may be the first source they consider. Therefore, it is wise that your etiquette with your attorney be nothing short of professional even if they are bogus. The reason being is that attorneys usually serve subtle purposes even after the case is over. For instance, let us say you may want a letter of recommendation for a parole consideration or a free copy of the trial record or if you need your attorney to testify to some mistake he or she made on appeal. What if the appellate court were to grant you an evidentiary hearing for some claim on your appeal and the victory of the appeal depended on something your attorney would have to acknowledge? You had better believe the attorney that sold you out despite your gracious and respectful disposition will be more inclined to help you than the one you slighted at every opportunity. If you were smart, you would maintain a good standing with your trial attorney because they may serve as the vital piece you need in the end.

Most of us come from environments where it is only natural to be upfront, direct, and in your face. In the streets, you don't have to hold your tongue or mince words. But this is not the streets, so those rules of engagement don't apply in this environment. The rules of engagement in the courtroom entails a much more professional, civilized, and tactical approach. In the courtroom, you must conduct yourself accordingly. I am not necessarily saying you must be someone you're not, and I am not telling you to be fake. But I am telling you to carry yourself by the ethics of the courtroom. There are ethics for when you play basketball in the gym, there is ethics for when you walk into any religious service, there is ethics in the workplace and there is ethics for courtrooms. This means anytime you come into the courtroom your disposition should be one of seriousness and respect. When talking, minimize your tone to blend in with the general tone of the rest of the room. How you walk, talk, the posture in which you even sit in your chair should all reflect you are an active participant in the process rather than just someone oblivious to the gravity of the situation. By projecting your humanity onto this process, it legitimizes it in such a way that affords you a relative degree of respect. In a sense, this even empowers you in ways you may not realize. To understand the rules of engagement, you must understand you cannot just blurt out something you feel the need to say during the proceedings. It involves you understanding if you want to address the judge, you must first have permission and when given permission, refer to the judge as 'your honor'. Moreover, it entails you conditioning yourself to speak in a much more formal fashion than you may be accustom. My very first time ever addressing the court, I remember accidentally using the phrase; you know what I'm saying. Now in hindsight, I laugh thinking about how green I was. At that point, I had not fully grasped courtroom etiquette. As mentioned earlier, the criminal justice system is set up in a way to project a sense of royalty onto judges however ridiculous and superficial it may come across. Even if addressing the judge by "your honor" seems foreign and lame, this is the ethics of the courtroom. For you to make the moves most conducive to your defense, you must conform to these rules of engagement. Otherwise, those overseeing this process will become an unnecessary hindrance. This process is not mechanical; or in other words, this process does not consist of invoking magical words that automatically bring about particular outcomes. This is not a video game. This system is run by a lot of obnoxious and arrogant people and obnoxious and arrogant people need validation. So just like anything else in life, the better you are with appealing to people's ego, the better your chances are these people will accommodate your requests. It's all about finding subtle ways to empower yourself in a situation that renders you powerless. This is relevant because there are some individuals who feel more empowered disrespecting the judge in this process. If that is your prerogative, by all intents and purposes, do you. However, in the grand scheme of things, what purpose does disrespecting the judge serve to someone needing the judge to make certain rulings in their favor? More than anything, disrespecting the judge displays one's ignorance and unfitness to win the war.

Everything in terms of etiquette and rules of engagement can be summed up in one word, finesse. If you have any type of finesse about yourself, implementing these rules of engagement should not be difficult. For the sake of this book, finesse is one's ability to adapt to any given situation in such a way that one does not appear to be out of their element. In this situation, finesse is imitating, mirroring, and mimicking legal jargon in a way that you distinguish yourself to be legally competent. There are individuals that literally spend years at law school studying legal terminology just to pass the Bar exam. It is unfortunate these individuals do not have the finesse we have; they do not realize the more effective you are with the art of mirroring, the faster you will begin familiarizing yourself with legal terminology. When I first started learning law, I started with my own case. I borrowed a copy of a motion previously filed by a licensed attorney and I copied the basic outline of that Motion. I had enough finesse to understand where I had to substitute my information and how I had to present my own claims apart from those the original attorney created. So no, I did not just copy another motion word for word; instead, I borrowed that motion's body structure and presentation. I borrowed that motions vocabulary. Then I implemented the facts of my case, argued my own points, used caselaw relative to my situation, and did so in such a way that it appeared to have come from an attorney. Such an approach is only advisable when you first start litigating. When you are learning how to draft motions, it is not plagiarism if you understand how to borrow only the presentation but implement your own demonstration.

When litigating, think about it like borrowing your friend's clothes, you would not borrow their underclothing, their boxer briefs, bra, or panties, you would only borrow their outer clothing, which is shirts or pants. This is how you should approach motions. To give you an example of what this means, in most States most motions will begin as such:

> *"Comes now the Movant, (name), pro se, and in good faith hereby moves this honorable court pursuant to Statute 439.240 J to order that (your request)."*

All motions filed in a Court of law will typically use this type of style to initiate the argument. Now for someone unfamiliar with the legal process, one would look at a motion and presume every word in the motion is a product of the individual who drafted it. The truth of the matter is legal jargon is so banal and conventional no one individual can take credit for this style of introduction. This style is standard for any legal motion in court. It wasn't unethical for me to borrow this style and add all my information and arguments that are relative to my situation. The objective is to refine one's legal motion in a manner that exhibits a semblance of conformity with the customary motions submitted by practitioners in the legal profession. Consequently, with repeated practice and extensive review of legal precedents, the process of drafting motions will progressively become more familiar to individuals. Over time, it will gradually develop into a state of being instinctive. Ultimately, you will progress to the point of competently applying legal terminology in motions in a way that is second nature. This is when you become finessed. This is particularly important, because finesse is something many defendants attempting to litigate law do not have. The reason they do not have it is due to not applying the right degree of finesse in their approach. Either they use too much finesse mirroring legal material with no true understanding of how to apply the law to their situation, or they do not use enough finesse by trying to litigate using no style or legal jargon whatsoever, but rather drafting their motions with the same style they use in everyday conversations. This is like somebody putting, "ya feel me" in their legal motion. This type of jargon will get you humiliated by both the judge and prosecutor.

There are two ways to present arguments to the judge during your case, oral and written/typed motions. An oral motion is an act of verbally articulating your arguments in the courtroom, on the record. Written/typed Motions are either handwritten or typed documents formally articulating one's request and your arguments in support thereof. If you are ever trying to present an Oral Motion to the Court, make sure to respect the rules of engagement. Which is not to blurt out during the court proceedings in a way that disrupts the natural order of the process. There is a specific order and form to every function in existence. The ethics for defendants in the criminal justice system are no different from ethics anywhere else. It is only by one's understanding of these ethics that Judges will acknowledge what you have to say in Court. This means you should respectfully ask permission from the Court before speaking; always remaining composed and civilized and always respecting all parties during the proceedings. It is custom in most courtrooms that defendants who are represented by an attorney do the least amount of speaking or addressing the court directly, to ensure they do not say something detrimental to their defense. Unless you have been officially granted the right to self-representation or some limited version of self-representation by the Judge, keep your oral communication in the Courtroom to a minimum and do all your communication to the judge in writing or with permission. For this reason, Oral Motions may not be the best option but rather the alternative. It may be better to file written/typed Motions. Pretrial motions[10] are generally standardized and basic across the board. If you do not have access to a computer, caselaw allows you to hand write these motions if they comply with the court rules in your state.

There are also rules of engagement when filing pretrial motions to the court. If you are drafting a motion on your own, it may be best to first write to the Clerk of the Court and request a free pro se self-help packet. All States usually provide a step-by-step outline of the Motion filing process in that state. Usually this will include prototypical motions and the different variables that are standard for your state when filing a motion to the court. If you follow all of the basic court rules, defendants need not worry too much about the format one uses to construct the motion, as judges will rarely deny a pretrial motion because of the incorrect structural format. Trial court judges are not as strict as appellate courts and will generally overlook minor deficiencies when filing pretrial motions.

When it comes time to file your pretrial motion, you should always acquire three copies. The first being the original copy you will send to the Clerk of the Court. And it may seem odd to send something meant for a judge to the clerk, but this is just formality. All Judges have clerks, who are like assistants and the job of a court clerk is to convey your motion to the Judge. The second copy of your motion goes to the prosecuting Attorney's office. The third copy you will keep for yourself for recording purposes. It is always safer to keep a copy of anything you file in the court, so if there is ever a discrepancy with it not getting there or about its contents, you have a copy at your disposal. Whenever you file a motion in court, it is mandatory in most states that you verify your motions by signing them and adding a proof of service clause with them. In some States, the rule requires certain motions to be notarized. Caselaw establishes that a valid service of process is necessary to assert personal jurisdiction over defendants. Courts generally require that a certificate of service be filed with the Court when a pleading, motion or other paper is served on the parties. Proof of service is a section attached to the motion outlining the who, what, when and where of the parties being served. This includes who the parties are, what the motion is, the date the Motion was mailed and where the motion was sent. This section will also need a signature. The following is an example of a typical proof of service necessary when filing motions to the court:

NOTICE

Please take notice that the foregoing and attached Motion to Vacate, Set aside, or Remand judgement has been filed in Division One of the Circuit Court via mailing the same to: Clerk of Trigg County Circuit Court at 41 Main St 42211-9143, P.O. Box 673, Cadiz, Kentucky 42211-0673 on this 32nd day of October 2022.

John Doe, Pro Se

CERTIFICATE OF SERVICE

This is to certify that a true and correct copy of the foregoing Motion has been mailed to: Trigg Commonwealth Attorney Prosecutors Office, Commonwealth Attorney Carrie L. Ovey-Wiggins, 248 Commerce St 42038, PO Box 679, Eddyville, Ky. 42038-0679 on this 32nd day of October 2022.

John Doe, pro se

It is imperative you learn to mirror legal etiquette with perfect finesse because you are dealing with a system seeking to impart fear through humiliation. The first rule of thumb in war is you must come into battle with absolute resoluteness; otherwise, you might squander the victory before the fighting even begins. This means you cannot go into this process scared. You were not sacred before you caught your case, so you should not be sacred now. Oftentimes, the very cause of fear is the ignorance we have about our circumstances. We do not fear what we identify with, but rather what we cannot identify with. This fear of the unknown is something we must get past because in this system there is no sympathy for our ignorance. In fact, in caselaw it is a clearly established legal principle that "ignorance of the law is no excuse". You will never be able to use that you didn't know as an excuse in a court of law.

The arrogant and vindictive nature of many judges and prosecutors anticipates any opportunity to humiliate, demean and dispirit defendants trying to exercise any semblance of legal competence. The law mandates Courts should liberally consider the pleadings of those unlettered in the law, but this system does not take this concept seriously because you are subject to the same standard as attorneys anytime you engage the court in "Pro Se[11] fashion. Therefore, your attempt to engage the court as if you belong there can possibly lead to harsh scrutiny. This is evident in caselaw, where a Judge, Justice Quirico, who was sitting as a single Justice of the Massachusetts Supreme Court Judicial Court, had a defendant brought into Court for the sole purpose of humiliating him as follows:

> *"Most of the documents prepared by the Petitioner and offered for filing can be best described as representing the indiscriminate, irrelevant and confusing use of legal jargon in attempted simulation of legal pleadings, with generous sprinklings of numerous references and citations (many of no applicability) to the United States and various Federal Court decisions, interspersed with quotations frequently taken out of context, from those opinions or from legal texts, and also with numerous Latin legal maxims thrown in for no discernible reason. Doubtless if*

> one were to comb through 263 pages of documents which the petitioner has thus far offered for filing, it might be possible somewhere therein to find various isolated statements which, if pieced together, might be worthy of consideration...." <u>Moore v. Massachusetts,</u> 674 F. Supp. 67.

The tone of the language in this case demonstrates the patronizing nature many judges and prosecutors will have with defendants who attempt to defend their personhood without an adequate degree of legal competency. To some degree, you cannot entirely blame the Courts for this frustration with legal incompetence. For instance, consider those who enjoy playing competitive basketball, if someone were to come on the basketball court with no semblance of basketball I.Q., no physical coordination, and no sense of how to play the game of basketball this would surely be irritating as it would disturb the competitiveness of the game. Someone passing themselves off to be something they are not would leave anyone frustrated and angry. The same logic applies to the court of law.

The true cause of fear comes from not knowing

the true nature of the thing you fear most. Sometimes removing this fear is a matter of just putting things in the proper perspective. Therefore, the best way to conquer fear of a particular thing is by finding something you fear more than that thing.

In a legal context, some of the things most defendants fear most are judges, legal terminology, and prosecutors. Nonetheless, the underlying element of all of these things is the prison sentence you are subject to if convicted. What you should fear more than anything is the nature of the prison sentence you are facing. Anyone fighting it out with the State should know exactly what the worst-case scenario is, necessitating you to have a firm grasp on your State penal code. For example, if you were to hold three people at gun point during a robbery, in Kentucky you could be charged with not just one, but three Counts of 1st Degree Robbery which holds 10 to 20 years in prison for each count. Therefore, in such a situation you would automatically know the worst-case scenario is going to trial and receiving 20 years for each Robbery charge leaving you with a 60-year sentence. This would be the worst- case scenario. Understanding the worst-case scenario provides you with the awareness to know what your options are and how you must further construct your defense. Failing to know the worst-case scenario blinds you from knowing the best-case scenario, further precluding you from making the right decisions.

6

"ALLIES OR ADVERSARIES?"

Interacting With Attorney's

"A lawyer appointed to represent a criminal defendant in a State Court proceeding is "as a matter of law, n o t a state actor." Such a lawyer, whether from the office of Public Advocacy or the Public Defender's Office is "no doubt, paid by government funds and hired by a government agency. Nevertheless, this function was to represent his client, not the interests of the State of the county. " It does not matter that a state criminal defense is paid from public funds. "Except for the source of payment, t h e duties

and obligations are the same whether [the client was} privately retained, appointed, or serving in a legal aid or defender program. This means that because a criminal defense lawyer's duty and loyalty are to his client, not to the State, a Court appointed attorney is not a state actor." (Skeakly v. Van De Mark, 2019 U.S. Dist. LEXIS 38188)

Allies are becoming increasingly a factor in modern warfare, as foreign alliances provide the more vulnerable countries with a means of security they would not otherwise have. As it stands, there is not a country without allies. For this reason, many of the wars in the future will most likely be world wars. Countries now must contemplate war under the assumption that such a decision amounts to war with all of that country's allies as well. This tells us before entering any war you must have an ally of some sort otherwise it could spell disaster. In this war you are fighting, that indispensable ally you must have is your attorney. Which makes the caselaw above conflicting because in a perfect world, court appointed attorneys should have their client's best interest at heart rather than the States, but unfortunately this is not a perfect world. In most situations, public advocates put their own interest first, which may sometimes render them vulnerable to the prosecutor's sway. Realistically, I cannot imagine anyone's dream job being that of an overworked and underpaid public advocate. For many attorneys, public advocacy jobs are either a last alternative or a stepping-stone to higher aspirations after law school, so as a result many public advocates are susceptible to leverage their clients in the name of advancing their career.

Nevertheless, not all public advocates are filthy, rotten, backstabbing, sellouts. In some cases, the insufficient representation provided by many public defenders is not malicious but a product of circumstance. Public defenders are incapable by default of affording any one defendant their full attention because of their enormous caseloads. It is impossible to help any one defendant prepare an adequate defense when they are also juggling 10 other defendants' cases as well. This massive caseload is a basis to conclude their overall representation could only be less than effective. For this reason, you should never entrust the entirety of your defense to your public advocate. You must have some idea of how you want to construct your defense. Regardless of how much experience your attorney has, you should develop a basic understanding of the law so you yourself are able to know whether your case warrants you to take a plea bargain, or whether you should go to trial. At the end of the day, you will have to do the time, not your attorney. Consequently, the purpose your attorney should serve is that of your legal advisor and mouthpiece. When you become finessed, you are then better suited to put the stirring wheel in their back. Meaning that you control everything they do; but this is only possible when you have a reasonable degree of how this legal process works. You can't demand to take control of the car if you don't know how to drive!

Once you have a firm grasp of this concept, an attorney can be your best asset even if it is a public advocate. Attorneys have always been an integral part of the justice system. Therefore, judges will always be more receptive to licensed attorneys. Why this is the case, I have no idea. I would imagine many judges feel it a slap in the face to have their profession they worked so hard to master, be exploited by those they deem degenerate criminals. This being the prevailing sentiment towards defendants charged with crimes. The attorney's true purpose in this process is to serve as buffers between you and the court. Unless your attorney is just so belligerent and uncooperative that you cannot get anything done through them, you should always try to utilize them for nothing more than the accessibility they provide.

One of the advantages of having an attorney act on your behalf in this process is that it provides you with a means to investigate certain matters you have no way of carrying out on your own. Investigations which include independent testing of DNA, GSR (gun-shot residue), drugs, interviewing witnesses, victims, and physical examinations of evidence such as weapons or crime scenes. If you are in jail while fighting your case, chances are there will be no one to carry out such tasks on your behalf. Having your attorney do this would be a lot cheaper than hiring a private investigator. However, this advantage is not absolute, so you must be reasonable when it comes to what you request to have investigated. Caselaw has granted attorneys the discretion to determine which investigations are valid and which are not. The United States Supreme Court has established:

> "[. .... Counsel has a duty to make reasonable investigations or to make a reasonable decision that makes a particular investigation unnecessary. In any ineffective case, a particular decision not to investigate must be directly assessed for reasonableness in all the circumstances, applying a heavy measure of deference to counsel's judgment." *(Strickland v. Washington,* 466 U.S. 668)

So again, anytime you feel it necessary for your attorney to investigate, it's best you explain to them exactly how it will be relative to your defense. Otherwise, the lawyer is not obliged to comply with your requests.

This idea of you guiding your attorney about which direction to take in your case is something most attorneys would eagerly embrace as it would relieve them of such work. However, no attorney would ever do anything at your request that would make them appear less than competent in the courtroom. Pretrial investigations require some form of convincing your attorney that what you're asking has merit. This necessitates some type of dialogue between yourself and your attorney, even if by letters. It may be best to correspond with your attorney through letters during the initial stages of the case. Establishing this line of communication is not always a terrible thing. Some communication is better than no communication. One must also keep in mind, all your attorney knows of you is your charges, so it may be that for them, the thought of face-to-face communication with somebody who would commit such a crime would be intimidating. If your attorney came to visit while terrified of you, chances are the meeting would not be as productive as you need it to be because they would be trying to get the meeting over with as quickly as possible. Whereas writing gives both parties all of the time and space necessary to express oneself in a way the other would be more receptive to. It also gives you an opportunity to make a positive impression in a way that you come off less intimidating. You will absolutely need to communicate face to face with your attorney weeks before trial time but any time before then it is not urgent. Writing your attorney should be something you make routine throughout the process.

Public defenders pose many problems for defendants, but as the saying goes, more money, more problems. By virtue of the money we pay private attorneys, it just may be that sometimes they end up being more of a headache than public defenders. In more cases than not, many private attorneys know early in a case whether it should be dismissed, pled out to, or taken to trial. This insight provides them with the necessary leeway to exercise the common ploy of prolonging cases for as long as possible. This ploy serves as a means of swindling as much money as they can from defendants. I call this 'legal ideate', **Pay as You Play** [12]. Attorneys apply this ploy by establishing an expectation from defendants of a substantial payment at every pretrial hearing. In most cases, attorneys can prolong a case for up to two years so this amounts to about four or five pretrial hearings, for which payments are expected. If this is not a racket, I do not know what is! This has led to attorneys hustling defendants out of large sums of money without ever providing a fair exchange of services. Attorneys will even withdraw from a case for bogus reasons after collecting their fees. Attorneys oftentimes get away with running this Pay as You Play racket because of the dynamic of the service they provide. We meet with attorneys wanting to acquire their services, often doing so through verbal agreement only. And a lot of times, attorneys will accept the terms of your verbal agreement, taking whatever money they can get on the spot but never establishing a set cost for their total representation. By not establishing a cost, this gives attorneys the flexibility to claim you failed to pay, without them having to reimburse you what you initially paid in advance. And when this happens what can you really do? When attorneys accept our verbal agreement, they do not provide us with contracts, receipts or invoices outlining an established agreement. Without proof of a receipt of service, payment arrangement, or binding contract enforcing an agreement, it becomes your word against theirs. I do not have to tell you what that entails in most cases. We make these agreements with attorneys on integrity, oblivious to the fact that there is no integrity in this system. When you violate the rights of others by breaking the law, society is not overly concerned with who violates your rights. This means you must protect yourself, even from those whose job it is to protect you. If you have the means to purchase the services of an attorney, you'd better transcribe the terms of your agreement, how much total for their representation and include a clause dictating that if the attorney does not uphold the agreement a full refund of your money is required. It does not have to be anything elaborate, just something that establishes a set price and the way you will pay and have your attorney sign it. This provides you with support if it happens that your attorney flips on you, thus providing some type of leverage to get your money back when filing a complaint to the BAR Association.

7

"A One-Man Army"

The Nuances of Self-Representation

Throughout history, there have been only a handful of fighters so gifted at combat that competing countries would bid for their service in times of war. This is the true definition of one-man armies. In the war you're fighting against the State, the closest thing there is to a one-man army is defendants who choose to represent themselves pro se. When a conflict arises with our attorney, we automatically consider self-representation the only solution. But self-representation is something you should never consider unless you have a substantial amount of experience with this process. As representing yourself pro se can be risky because when you waive your constitutional right to representation, in some but not all instances, you could cut yourself off from one of the more common arguments on appeal, which is ineffective assistance of counsel claims.

Anytime you make a request to represent yourself pro se, the Court is required to conduct a full **Faretta hearing.** [13] At this hearing, most judges will always try to convince defendants why self-representation is not in their best interest. Nevertheless, caselaw establishes the Court's primary responsibility at these Faretta hearings is not merely to offer you their advice but to *"confirm that a defendant's decision to proceed pro se involves a knowing and intelligent waiver of the Federal constitutional right to counsel."* This hearing is basically a waiver hearing.

> *The idea method of assuring that a waiver is valid is for the trial court to conduct a pretrial [Faretta] hearing at which the accused is informed of the charges, basic trial procedures, and hazards the accused is informed of the charges, basic trial procedures, and hazards of self-*

representation.

United States v. Owen, 963 F.3d 1040 (11ᵗʰ Cir. 2020)

However, pro se representation is a very flexible legal concept. A defendant acting pro se in the truest sense is one that relies on zero assistance from any licensed attorneys at all but does everything on their own. This degree of pro se representation is rare, as many defendants are unable to sustain this high level of pro se representation due to not knowing every nuance of the legal process. And those who can sustain this type of pro se representation from beginning to end will lose the ability to argue any claims of ineffective assistance of counsel by virtue of not having an attorney throughout the process. The next degree of pro se is the self-representation of the defendant accompanied by the help of stand by counsel. A petitioner in <u>United States v. Cargill,</u> 2022 U.S. App. LEXIS 26519 sums up this degree of pro se beautifully. In this case, the Petitioner addresses the court with the following:

"I'm requesting the right to self-representation and moving my

right to Sixth Amendment ... counsel but at the same time requesting to work with co-counsel to take on the more difficult parts or the tactical parts of the procedure such as Federal rules of Evidence and helping with the objections and tactical parts."

Those that sustain this degree of pro se representation will also forfeit many ineffective assistance of counsel claims, depending on the extent that standby counsel assisted them throughout the process. The last degree of pro se one can exercise is the self-representation of the defendant as co-counsel alongside their attorney. And I have personal experience with this degree of self-- representation as it is only available in a handful of States, one being Kentucky. Someone I knew very well, made the decision to start learning how this legal process works, and thereby had to learn through trial and error that the United States Constitution only requires Faretta hearings for those that specifically articulate the intent to proceed <u>pro se.</u> This means the Appellate courts have determined that asking to represent yourself, as your own co-counsel does not equate to requesting to represent yourself pro se. When you ask to represent yourself as your own co-counsel, you are invoking a State right. If that right is violated only the State appellate court can provide you with relief. Whereas if you ask to represent yourself pro se, you are invoking your federal right, so if the trial Court violates this right, you can later petition the federal court for relief. This was my very first lesson in understanding that anytime you invoke a right in court, you must articulate what Constitution and amendment protects that right.

8

"THE PEACE TREATY AGREEMENT"

Approaching Plea Bargains

Not every war culminates with a winner and loser. Sometimes, there are instances where the casualties sustained during a war are so fatal that even if one were to win the war, it would be to no effect. For example, Ukraine has opted to go to war to prevent the foreign invasion of Russia, but in the process of the war, if Ukraine's landscape were to sustain so much geographical damage rendering it uninhabitable, could Ukraine really deem that a win. Even if Ukraine were to win such a war, the damage sustained in doing so would render it a loss. This is the proverbial concept known as a Pyric Victory. To prevent falling into such a trap, you must always see the bigger picture. Is your one and only goal the satisfaction to say you beat the case? Or is the goal freedom and getting home to your family in the least amount of time possible? If it is freedom, taking a guilty plea might be the wisest thing you can do. For whatever reason, there has been a negative stigma around taking guilty pleas. Perhaps as risk takers, we frown on the idea of 'copping out' stemming from an unrealistic all or nothing mentality. This all or nothing mentality might be the right approach when gambling; but this is not the right mentality to have when fighting for your life. The only way to understand this is by understanding the fundamental role of plea bargains in this system, as defined by caselaw. In <u>Missouri v. Frve,</u> 566 U.S. 134, the United States Supreme Court established that,

> *"Because ours is for the most part a system of pleas, not a system of trials.... It is insufficient simply to point to the guarantee of a fair trial as a backstop that inoculates any errors in the pretrial process. To a large extent. Horse trading between prosecutor and defense counsel determines who goes to jail and for how long. That is what plea bargaining is. It is not some adjunct to the criminal justice*

> *system; it is the Criminal Justice System. Defendants who do take their case to trial and lose receive longer sentences than even Congress or the prosecutor might think appropriate, because the longer sentences exist on the books largely for bargaining purposes. This often results in individuals who accept a plea bargain receiving shorter sentences than other individuals who are less morally culpable but take a chance and go to trial. In today's Criminal Justice System, therefore, the negotiation of a plea bargain, rather than the unfolding of a trial, is almost the most critical point for a defendant."*

This caselaw demonstrates how the criminal justice system undeniably indorses the idea of over sentencing defendants who opt to go to trial, as a deterrent not to go to trial. This is something you should factor into your decision. We are dealing with a system that does not try to hide the fact that if you go to trial and lose, they are going to over sentence you. There is a certain approach you must have in fighting a case and deciding whether to take a plea. This approach hinges on whether you are innocent, justified, or guilty. If you are one of the few individuals that are innocent, then no, you should never, under any circumstance, accept a plea of guilty. I guess that's easy to say if I am not the one on trial, but my logic is that by accepting a plea of guilty you are abandoning your one and only opportunity to prove your innocence. How can you argue you were wrongfully convicted if you never attempted to assert your innocence? I can only tell you what any innocent person should do under the circumstances, which is, stand on your innocence at trial and put your trust in the idea that the truth will prevail.

The plea-bargaining process is essentially a negotiation. Therefore, if you happen to be outright guilty, and you know that going to trial is not your best option you should first ascertain how much **bargaining power** [14] you possess in this process. This 'legal ideate' regarding one's bargaining power comprises two things: 1). The amount of Subjective Doubt that exists as to your guilt at face value, and 2). The Evidentiary Conviction Probability (E.C.P). In terms of the first element, when considering the Subjective Doubt that exists, always remember, prosecutors are not super humans who know whether you committed the crime or not. They are no different from anyone else; they consider the particulars and evidence and from that, they reach a speculative conclusion using their common sense, knowledge and understanding. The keyword in the last sentence is speculative. This means that unless you give a confession, a prosecutor could never know if you are guilty with 100% certainty but has only an idea. And even if the prosecutor does think you're guilty, there is always that small probability of your innocence; that small doubt that exists in the back of their mind. And it is this very doubt that provides you with your bargaining power. Again, prosecutors are human beings too, though they will not admit it, deep down there is always a fear of whether they're prosecuting an innocent person no matter how small that doubt may be. The stronger this fear and doubt, the more inclined they are to offer you a plea bargain, and sometimes a prosecutor's plea is not about just securing a conviction, sometimes prosecutors need the relief of knowing for themselves whether their speculation is correct or not. The more you and your attorney can leverage the evidence in a way that creates some doubt in the prosecutor's mind, the more likely you are to procure the most favorable guilty plea. For the guilty, your bargaining power will dictate if you should take a guilty plea at all and if so, what the plea should look like.

The second component of your bargaining power is what I call *E.C.P.* [15] Keep in mind, every move the prosecutor makes is trial-oriented, even in cases they know are unlikely to go to trial. The quality of any plea you receive will most likely be based on what I call the Evidentiary Conviction Probability, which is a determination of how strong the evidence is against you combined with the probability of that evidence translating into your conviction at trial. The reason E.C.P's are so important is sometimes a mountain of evidence does not always translate to an automatic conviction. There are certain obstacles that stand to threaten the evidence prosecutors have against you such as **the Rules of Evidence** [16]. Prosecutors often deal with evidentiary mishaps causing a Judge to rule certain types of **evidence inadmissible**[17] at trial. Defendants should always make it a point to familiarize oneself thoroughly with the Rules of Evidence in your State. There are also factors that may occur that do not outright justify a criminal offense but may mitigate the punishment. All of which contribute to the probability of you being convicted.

Prosecutors come in all different forms, so your plea negotiations will reflect the type of prosecutor you have. To understand the wide discretion prosecutors have in such situations, you must first understand the caselaw relative to such. Prosecutors serve as the principal advocates of the almighty State, having a wide range of latitude. The United States Supreme Court outlines in <u>Wayte v. United States,</u> 470 U.S. 598 how,

> "In our Criminal Justice System, the government retains" broad discretion as to whom to prosecute. <u>United States v. Goodwin.</u> 457 US 368, 380, n. 11(1987); <u>Marshall v. Jerricho. Inc.</u>• 446 US 278, 248 (1980) "[So] long as the prosecutor has probable cause to believe that the accused committed an offense defined by statute, the decision whether or not to prosecute and what charge to file or bring before a Grand Jury, generally rests entirely in his discretion." <u>Bordenkircher v. Hayes.</u> 43.J U.S. 357, 364(/978), This broad discretion rest largely on the recognition

that this decision to prosecute is particular ill-suited to judicial review. Such factor such as the strength of the case, the general deterrence value, the governments enforcement priorities, and the cases relationship to the Governments overall enforcement plan are not readily susceptible to the kind of analysis the courts are competent to undertake. Judicial supervision in this area, moreover, entails systemic costs of particular concern. Examining the basis of a prosecution delays the criminal proceedings. threatens to chill law enforcement by subjecting the prosecutor's motives and decision-making to outside inquiry and may undermine prosecutorial effectiveness by revealing the Governments Enforcement policy. All these are substantial concerns that make the courts hesitant to examine the decision whether to prosecute."

The impact of this language shows itself in the fact that this case appears 1,876 times from 1985 to 2022 in both Federal and State Appellate caselaw. This very language more than likely serves to deny countless defendant's relief from prosecutorial misconduct claims. This alone should give you an idea of the type of power being afforded to prosecutors in this process. Prosecutors have the discretion to decide who to charge, what to charge or whether to charge at all.

When negotiating with someone with this type of leverage, it is necessary to utilize every clue possible to gain an advantage in the negotiation process. Anytime the prosecutor offers you a plea, it should also serve as a means of intel; I call this legal **ideate Plea Styling** [18]. Plea Styling involves scrutinizing a plea from the prosecution as a means of ascertaining the disposition and degree of interest the State has in acquiring your personhood.

For example, if a prosecutor's first offer is a 5-year plea bargain for a charge that holds a maximum of 20 years, this suggests that you are not a high priority of the State. While some may take this to imply a lack of evidence, this is something you must be very, very careful with, as you must never mistake mercy for weakness. I once knew someone who refused to take a 9-year plea for a charge that held life. This individual proceeded to trial and ultimately received life on that case and died in prison still fighting to get out after having served over 25 years. Therefore, a lenient plea may not always be the product of an inability to bring about a conviction. It just may be mercy.

While on the other hand, sometimes a lenient plea is exactly that, an omission of weakness. Prosecutors are conscious of the advantageous position they enjoy in this situation. Many understand the odds are stacked against defendants in a way that makes it difficult to prevail in trial. So as arrogant as many prosecutors are, they will generally save face rather than be potentially embarrassed by defeat in trial. Every prosecutor's deepest fear is taking a defendant to trial, confident to bring about a conviction, only to come out on the losing side. They dread experiencing this type of inadequateness and incompetence. They fear experiencing the embarrassment of having to explain to the victim's family why they were not able provide justice. More hurtful than that is the disappointment, lack of confidence, and dishonor they fear receiving from their own co- workers, peers, and superiors. Whether contrived or not, this is a feeling prosecutors frantically seek to avoid. To circumvent this emotional catastrophe, prosecutors will offer those charged with some of the most egregious crimes the most favorable plea bargains not as tokens of leniency, but a means to save the State the embarrassment of holding a trial they know cannot be won. Which is ironic because in any case where the E.C.P is high, most prosecutors will offer excessive plea bargains hoping that defendants opt to go to trial so they can make an example of them. In these types of situations, these excessive pleas will be in nature something like what a defendant would receive in trial if found guilty. For those such as myself who have been in this situation, the logic and mentality becomes one of martyrdom, because if defeat is inevitable, why not make the State deplete its funds in the process.

In most States, prosecutors will typically offer a defendant two plea offers before taking the idea of a trial serious. As all communication and bargaining is done through your attorney, it will be your attorney who can best provide you with a feel of the prosecution's intentions for your case. However, until you trust your attorney, be careful about exposing your actual intentions. Because let's just say the prosecutor offers you a plea and you inform your attorney you want to hold out for a better plea and that you really have no intention of going to trial. If it happens that your attorney is a rat, backstabbing, sell-out he could go and convey this information to the prosecutor who would then have the leverage to sit on that first offer knowing you're going to eventually cave in and take the plea. You must never expose your true intentions even to your attorney until after you get the plea you're willing to accept. You must maintain your poker face when your attorney conveys a plea offer from the prosecutor. Never appear too anxious for a deal and never convey to your attorney if the conditions of the jail are weighing on you because this is also an element prosecutors use to prompt you to take a less than favorable deal.

Consistent with any negotiation tactic in business, the first plea offer from a prosecutor is always a feeler. If you have any type of leverage and bargaining power in the negotiation, the first offer should not be taken seriously, but you should always present a reply offer the prosecutor can use as a feeler. The second offer from the prosecutor should be a compromise between the first and your reply offer. If the prosecutor is taking the negotiation seriously, the second offer and any thereafter is something you should also consider with seriousness. It is only your leverage and bargaining power that allows you to take this negotiation any further than this. One can only hope your attorney is an astute negotiator or rather negotiate on your behalf at all. I am of the idea defendants should involve themselves more in the plea negotiating process as much as possible, which entails establishing some type of communication between you, your attorney, and the prosecutor. As this is not always possible, if there is a situation that you do not trust your attorney and feel like their trying to railroad you, it may be wise to write a letter to the judge requesting to have all plea offers from the prosecution sent to both you and your attorney for "purposes of preserving the record for appeal". As crazy as it sounds, there have been attorneys who failed to convey to their client favorable pleas offered by prosecutors. The Federal Courts have expressed that,

> *"The attorney has a clear obligation to fully inform her client of the available options. We have held that*

> *the failure to convey a plea offered constitutes ineffective assistance of counsel." <u>Griffin v. United States</u>, 330 F.3d 733 Also, in, <u>Smith v. United States</u>, 3-18 F.3d 545, "an evidentiary hearing l-VGS was granted as to whether a defendant would have pleaded guilty where attorney failed to convey a plea offer of five years and the defendant was subsequently sentenced to 156 months."*

A handwritten letter asking the Court to direct the prosecutor to deliver any plea bargains to you would demonstrate your due diligence. This is not to imply that you should be paranoid and start accusing your attorney of withholding plea offers without a sufficient basis, because in most cases attorneys will convey this information out of ethical duty. This is also not to imply that you should engage in negotiations with prosecutors without an attorney present for the simple reason that prosecutors are susceptible to use any and everything you say against you in this process. Communication with prosecutors without a third party is never a good idea because what you do not want is for what started out as a plea negotiation to end up as an indictment on more charges.

As mentioned in the beginning, there is this sentiment going around that going to trial, regardless of the circumstances, is the right thing to do. This is the furthest thing from the truth. For those that are guilty, going to trial is like trying to fight off somebody robbing you at gunpoint. Sometimes it's just not worth it. When somebody has the drop on you, the mentality you should have is to yield what you have until you are in a better position to get it back. If you happen to die trying not to be robbed, what chance do you have then of recovering what you lost? During any robbery, the goal is to get out of the situation alive. Pride should never seal your fate. Just as pride should never keep you from turning down a reasonable plea deal only to get double or triple that in trial. You must apply the risk versus reward test to such decisions. Does the reward of knowing you got away with something outweigh the risk of losing your freedom for decades? If there is anything you love more than yourself, it should not. For many of us, especially first-time offenders, there is this aspiration of not wanting to take any deal. This unrealistic expectation of wanting to walk away scot-free is naive if not ignorant. If you are lucky enough that something in your case is so flawed it warrants you walking away with no sentence at all, many judges will try everything in their power to remedy it in a way that does not amount to them having to dismiss the case. There are but a number of instances judges dismiss cases before trials; these include double jeopardy violations, lack of jurisdiction violations, and cases involving self-defense. These situations are all civil liabilities, meaning they all subject the state to civil lawsuits. Though dismissals happen from time to time, these types of situations are as rare as hitting the Powerball. As mentioned earlier, we gamble with our freedom as if it is just a random hand in a poker game. We fail to realize the greatest risk takers do not depend on blind luck. The risk takers we see at high stakes poker games are often mathematicians who can shrewdly assess the probabilities of the risks they take. Such individuals are keenly familiar with mathematical percentages, probabilities and algorithms enabling them to play the best odds, thus providing them with the best chances of winning. Deciding whether to go to trial is not about taking chances with no understanding of the risks, it is about playing the best possible odds. So as a defendant, you should always ask yourself, realistically, what are my chances of losing at trial? You must factor everything such as the resources you have or do not have, whether you have a paid trial attorney or public defender, the evidence against you, the E.C.P in your case, the strength of your pretrial plan, how much time your actually facing, how much of your life you stand to lose, and whether you have a defensive theory worth arguing. One's strategy in trial should never just be to wish upon a mistrial or something happening during the trial you can use on appeal. This is tantamount to going into a shootout with nothing but hope that your enemy has a bad aim.

    None of this is an attempt to convince you to cop out, but only to warn you about everything you best consider before making such a decision. I'm just helping you to cover all your bases. This is my attempt to provide you with a clear and logical perspective, rather than just telling you what you want to hear. In the process of making such decisions, rarely will you get sound advice from other individuals. The advice you even get from your family should come secondary to what is best for you. Because everyone is inclined to look at your situation through the prism of their personal understanding, advising you based on their interests. Such is not the standard you should use when making your decision. Such is not the standard you should use to make any decision. The standard should always be one of logic.

One of the reasons people feel reluctant to take a plea even when they are guilty is because there may be something they believe they can argue on appeal. If ever you're put in a situation where a plea is in your best interest, but there is something in your case worth appealing, a conditional plea is your best course of action. Conditional plea [19] stems from the federal court but are something some States will recognize under certain conditions. To be sure, research caselaw in your respective State to see what the rule is with conditional guilty pleas. The Federal Rules of Criminal Procedure State 11(c)(2) states:

> *"With the consent of the Court and the government, a defendant may enter a conditional plea of guilty or nolo contender, reserving in writing the right to have an appellate Court review an adverse determination of a specified pretrial motion. A defendant who prevails on appeal may then withdraw the plea."*

It was further outlined in <u>United States v. Bundy,</u> 392 F. 3d 641, 645(4th Cir. 2004) that:

> *"We have explained that the writing requirement "ensure[s] careful attention to any conditional plea and [makes] plain to the parties and the court 'that a particular plea was in fact conditional' as well as 'precisely what pre-trial issues have been preserved for appellate review.*"

As mentioned above, a conditional plea is a plea you accept that allows you to appeal specific issues that occur in the pretrial phase of the case. Such a plea bargain is not absolute. Before you can receive this form of plea, both the Court and prosecutor must agree upon it before it can be valid. Once agreed upon, the agreement must clearly outline which issues you seek to discuss on appeal; otherwise, the appellate Court will deny it.

Conditional pleas are necessary because any time you accept a plea agreement, under the law, you automatically waive your right to appeal in your case. Anytime you take a plea, there is always what is called plea-colloquy at the final sentencing hearing in which the judge makes you aware of the consequences of taking the plea by engaging you directly, essentially inquiring into if you're entering into the plea in a knowing and voluntarily state. At this time, you should raise any concern you have because in many cases, prosecutors will convey certain promises in **plea agreements** [20] or through attorneys, that the Department of Corrections will ultimately refuse to enforce once your sentence begins. These situations include matters such as jail credit, how your sentence is to run with another sentence or parole eligibility. Prosecutors are often aware that regardless of what they outline in your plea agreement, the Department of Corrections will only acknowledge what is in your final judgment as well as what your State penal code requires. So never ever, rely solely on what prosecutors write in your plea agreement, but always make sure any conditional pleas or promises made from the prosecution are valid under **State law, part of the record during your plea colloquy and/or included in your final judgement** [21].

9

"THE BEST OFFENSE IS A GOOD DEFENSE"

The Importance of Having a Defense

In war, sometimes victory is contingent on which side can produce the most effective strategy. For defendants, the more effective your defensive strategy, the more energy your adversary will exert trying to offset it thereby sidetracking them from the goal, which is winning. In this process, the defendant with no defense provides the prosecutor the luxury of remaining in attack mode. In attack mode, prosecutors will seek superseding indictments, higher pretrial bail, as well as more excessive prison sentences. Every move the prosecutor makes in a case correlates with the defense they anticipate you will present at trial. In the absence of a defense, the prosecution has the luxury of focusing on ways to strengthen its case against you rather than worrying about defending their own. You must approach this situation as the chess game it is. In some cases, simply having any strategy is better than no strategy because it provides you an opportunity to bluff. If you can make the prosecutor believe that your defense is formidable, even if it is not, this increases the likelihood of them offering you a favorable plea agreement. But this can only be possible by establishing your defense as earliest as possible in a case. The question you should ask yourself is what is my defense [22]?

This idea of having a defense may seem contradictory to what I have previously stated earlier, but this is not the case. My emphasizing that every defendant must always have a defense does not mean that you should not still have an offensive mentality throughout this process. The legal term, defense, merely describes what strategy you are utilizing to defend yourself at trial rather than any type of fixed position one is assigned such as with sports. This means, even as the defendant, you should still have an offensive mentality in proving your case and the only way to do this is through your defense. In this system, criminal charges are comprised of elements, which must be proven before one can be guilty of any charge. Charges like robbery and burglary are broken down into specific elements that make up those charges. The standard for prosecutors to prove a particular charge, entails proving defendant's actions correlates with the element of that charge. This requires prosecutors to have an offensive mentality when proving these elements. Similarly, defenses are also made up of elements. The basis for proving you are innocent of the charge correlates with you proving each element of the defense that offsets that charge. Therefore, for every charge, there will also be a particular defense to offset it. In essence, both a defendant and the prosecutor each have a set of elements to substantiate. Therefore, both should be in offensive mode as well as defensive at times.

The United States Constitution provides you the

right to present a complete defense. In this situation, it is not enough just to present any defense; but victory requires that you present the right defense. There are countless defenses but really the only defenses the court will acknowledge are those that caselaw approves.

The most common defenses to charges are Affirmative defenses, Imperfect defenses, and Perfect defenses. Affirmative defenses comprise a set of elements that either justify or excuse the accused, even if a prosecutor can prove all of the elements of the charge. Affirmative defenses include self-defense in all its various forms, insanity defenses, low-IQ defenses and defenses of duress involved in civil lawsuits. When you employ any Affirmative defense, the court places the burden on you to prove that the elements justify your actions rather than prosecutors having to prove any type of elements. Next are Imperfect defenses. Imperfect defenses are those that include a set of elements, which assert that though you may be guilty, it is only of a lesser charge. Imperfect defenses include lesser evils defenses, men's rea or State of Mind defenses, and intoxication defenses. Imperfect defenses also include imperfect self-defense, which involves a set of elements proving you are guilty of a lesser charge because your intent was a lesser form of self-defense. Imperfect defenses are defenses that require the prosecutor to prove your guilt rather than you having to prove the elements of the defense. But again, you must never, ever fall into the trap of believing that you don't have to prove your innocence. By default, juries unconsciously presume anything that prosecutors say to be fact, unless a defendant can provide an alternative they can reasonably conceive. By any account, jurors will never truly relieve you of having to disprove the prosecution's case in some way, shape or form regardless of what the court admonishes them to do. This is just human nature. Always go about the business of knowing and proving the elements of your defense regardless of any question of burden of proof. Next are Perfect Defenses. Perfect Defenses are those that involve a set of elements that warrant an automatic acquittal of the charges. Perfect Defenses includes exculpatory defenses, **ostrich defenses**[23], derivative defenses [24], and actus reus defenses. [25]

Establishing your defense at the onset of your case

sets the tone by way of conveying to the prosecutor that you understand what elements you need to meet to prevail, that you have a strategy to prove those elements at trial and that you are willing to execute that plan if necessary. This outwardly projects to prosecutors that you have a sense of confidence in what you're doing even if that is not the case. Alternatively, if you are the defendant approaching this process with no defense or with a defense that courts do not acknowledge, prosecutors will immediately see this as a weakness and as an invitation to be as aggressive as possible? Every request you make to the judge, every pretrial motion, every pretrial hearing you attend should all be to place yourself in the best possible position to prevail at trial. Every court rule, caselaw or statue you research and plan to exercise should all be to strengthen your defense. Every meeting you have with your attorney, every piece of evidence you have tested or examined should all be to strengthen your defense. If this were a game of poker; your defense would be your bargaining chips. You could come to the poker table with all of the trial strategies in the world, but what good would it do if you don't have the necessary chips to play. For instance, if you are being charged with robbery, what good does it do for your defense to prove that the whole incident was a "drug deal gone bad" if there are no such instructions or elements to get you off the charge? The reason there is no instructions for such a defense is that 'a drug deal gone bad' is not a defense to the charge of Robbery. In fact, "a drug deal gone bad" is not a defense to any charge because there is no 'drug deal gone bad instructions' providing the elements to prevail on this defense. So how could a jury even take such a defense serious? The only defenses juries are receptive to are those they have instructions for when they deliberate. For example, when a defendant's defense at trial is self-defense, the jury has a specific 'self-defense jury instruction' with a particular set of elements that avail the defendant if the elements are met. This instruction provides the elements for juries to apply to the defendant's defense. In cases where a defendant argues intoxication as a defense for murder, there is a specific 'intoxication jury instruction' provided to the jury outlining the elements in a way juries are able to apply to the case. What this means is the validity of your defense depends on whether the jury will have instructions to even consider it.

If you pay attention, prosecutors will always make sure the trial court approves of the strategy they intend to present before trial. Prosecutors do this by invoking certain court rules and requesting the Court to admit certain evidence into the record right before trial begins. Therefore, this is something defendants must also do. This means that before trial, you must present to the Court what your defense will be and whether it is one the court deems legitimate. The wisdom of having the Court acknowledge and validate your defense going to trial provides you an opportunity of having the Court issue specific jury instructions [26] that correlate to your defense.

The Federal Court has established that,

> *"In order to successfully assert a defense in a criminal trial, "it is sufficient that the defendant have shown an 'underlying evidentiary foundation' as to each element of the defense, regardless of how weak, inconsistent, or dubious' the evidence on a given point may seem."*
> United States v. Kabat, 797 F. 2d

at 590-91(8th Cir. 1986) (quoting United States V. Gross, 650 F. 2d 1336, 1345(5th Cir. 1981).

The case above actually dictates that a defendant has a right to present any defense if there is some type of evidence in the case supporting it. If the law were to apply the way it literally reads above, a defendant facing a robbery charge could in fact present a defense of a 'drug deal gone bad', if there was some type of evidence to support and avail one of the charges. The Court would then have to permit the jury to consider 'drug deal gone bad instructions' with elements that would alternately avail a defendant of the Robbery charge. However, as I have mentioned before, the law is not as black and white as it may appear. Courts often interpret law in a manner that favors the State. Courts will typically not consider any other defenses other than those caselaw acknowledges. But this could very well be an issue worthy of having an appellate court consider.

10

"BROTHER IN ARMS"

The Dynamics of Co-Defendants

In our culture, we stigmatize the idea of having a rap partner or a co-defendant. The reason being is in far too many instances, prosecutors are strong-arming cases through the tactic of divide and conquer. Those who come into the system with a codefendant immediately feel the anxiety of not knowing what their codefendant will do in the case. After months and months of sitting in jail, this paranoia often results in defendants convincing themselves that their co-defendants will turn on them; this provides the incentive and self-justification to beat their co-defendants to the punch. All of the while, their co-defendant may never have even entertained such an idea. Or, in the interrogation room, officers may insinuate that your co-defendant has already made statements against you when that may not be the case. Both police officers and prosecutors are often successful at applying the divide and conquer tactic because they are keenly aware of which defendants will likely succumb to an opportunity to lessen their sentence at the expense of their codefendant. The logic of the State is if they can pressure one of any of the defendants to acknowledging their theory of facts [27] during the trial in exchange for a favorable plea, this in effect paralyzes and undermines any theory the remaining defendants could then present. Which is true, because regardless of the ulterior motives that exist for defendants to testify against their codefendant, juries will always give momentous weight to your co-conspirator's testimony. Most juries that approach criminal cases believe the majority of those charged with crimes are most likely guilty. Therefore, the testimony of a codefendant is equivalent to a guilty confession. So inversely, this could only mean that co-defendants that do not "flip" on one another holding fast to the same defense may stand a better chance. The logic behind this premise is that juries rely on theories of facts to determine guilt or acquittal. Anything that might even remotely convey an iota of doubt to a jury is significant. Depending on the situation, if codefendants could withstand the pressures of double-crossing one another, and collectively present a plausible defense while also testifying to an identical theory of facts, this could be a determining factor in coming out on the winning side of this war. One of the few ways defendants can produce some degree of doubt is through maintaining a substantial degree of consistency throughout this process. Such consistency shown by both defendants may provide juries with a basis to begin developing the infamous 'reasonable doubt' [28]. But for this idea to even have a chance, co-defendants would have to implement this tactic as early as possible in the case. This means, there should be a plausible consistency of the facts conveyed by each defendant, starting first with the post arrest interrogation, the probable cause hearing, evidentiary hearings, and finally testimony at trial. If all defendants consistently maintain the same theory of facts throughout this entire process, this is something factfinders will instinctively factor into its deliberation. This idea should or could never suffice as one's sole strategy of defense at trial, but again, in certain situation(s) this could serve as a determining factor tipping the balance in the defendant's favor.

The criminal justice system considers all defendants indistinguishable. If you catch a case and are a prime candidate for probation, diversion, or deferred prosecution, but your co-defendant has an extensive record subjecting him to the prosecutor's wrath; it just may happen that you inadvertently catch the same wrath as your co-defendant. In some instances, it may be wise to disassociate yourself as much as possible from your co-defendant. You can do this without having to testify against a co-defendant by simply requesting that the Court sever you and your co-defendants' trials. In legal terms, this would require you to file a Motion for Severance during pretrial. As something that can potentially benefit defendants, prosecutors will routinely argue against it and most judges will naturally oppose it. The general standard to prove when arguing for a Severance of trial from your co-defendant is whether *"the sheer volume and magnitude of the evidence against one defendant so dwarfs the proof presented against his codefendant that a severance is required to prevent unacceptable spillover prejudice."*

This may not be the exact standard in each State, but the standard in your respective State will be very similar to this. When arguing this motion, you should also demonstrate how the court's failure to grant this request would somehow violate a constitutional right of yours, which increases your chances of having it granted. In any situation where your co-defendant has an overwhelming amount of evidence against him but for whatever reason that is not the case with you, a Severance of trial is probably something you should consider filing.

11

"CLASSIFIED INTEL"

The Purpose of Discovery

"We have elected to employ an adversary system of criminal justice in which the parties contest all issues before a court of law. The need to develop all relevant facts in the adversary system is both fundamental and comprehensive. The ends of criminal justice would be defeated if judgments were to be found on a partial or speculative presentation of facts. The very integrity of the judicial system and public confidence in the system depend on full disclosure

> *of all the facts, within the framework of the rules of evidence. To ensure that justice is done, it is imperative to the function of courts that compulsory process be available for the production of evidence needed either by the prosecution or by the defense.* "<u>United States v. Nixon,</u> 418 U.S. 683, 709 (1974)

For defendants, the decision-making process as to what route to take in a case should not begin until you have reviewed your entire discovery. **Your discovery** [29] is the record of all of the evidence there is against you. In every case, the prosecutor will always give you a few glimpses of how thorough their case is against you and that tell-sign is your discovery. The discovery in any case is usually available to the defendant around 2-4 months after the grand jury issues an indictment. At this time, the prosecutor will send your attorney a copy of the discovery, which your attorney should then forward to you. It is a rule of thumb that prosecutors must generally disclose any evidence they intend to use against you in trial. The reason being is that defendants must be given adequate time to test or examine such evidence, if necessary. This means you do not have to worry about the prosecution bombarding you at trial with something unexpected. And if the prosecution happens to surprise you at trial with something that has not been disclosed to you prior to trial, this is often grounds to ask for a continuance or even a mistrial. Black's Law Dictionary Ninth Edition defines mistrial as, *"A trial that the judge brings to an end, without a determination on the merits, because of a procedural error or serious misconduct occurring during the proceedings. Or a trial that ends inconclusively because the jury cannot reach a verdict."*

Something to keep in mind is the bigger your discovery, the more developed the prosecution's theory will likely be at trial; and the smaller your discovery, the less developed it will likely be. One's discovery is typically comprised of police reports, criminal complaints, victim statements, witness statements, police statements, forensic testing, photos of the physical evidence, police evidence room logs, post arrest statements made by the accused, hospital records, photos of the victims' injuries, photos of the accused, crime scene photos, etc. All of which paint a picture of what the prosecutor's case will be against you. Of all of the evidence in your discovery, the most important will always be the exculpatory evidence the prosecution provides, if any exists. Exculpatory evidence is any evidence favorable to the accused. United States Supreme Court Caselaw entitled, <u>Brady v. Maryland,</u> 373 U.S. 83, provides,

> *"The Suppression by the prosecution of evidence favorable to an accused upon request violates due process where the evidence is material either to guilt or to punishment, irrespective of the good faith or bad faith of the prosecution.*

This means that if any evidence with the potential to prove your innocence is lost or destroyed, the constitution requires that it may warrant the dismissal of the charges against you. This requires both police officers and prosecutors to disclose any evidence they come across that so happens to be material or favorable to your defense. Caselaw in <u>Ariz v. Youngblood,</u> 488 U.S. 51, provides that aside from just exculpatory evidence, defendants are also entitled to *potentially* exculpatory evidence.

> *".. When evidence in question is only potentially useful, as opposed to clearly exculpatory, a criminal defendant who claims destruction of evidence violated his due process rights must prove the police were acting in bad faith when the evidence was destroyed."*

Black's law Dictionary 9th Edition defines bad faith as, "Dishonesty of belief or purpose." This means that to succeed on a claim regarding potentially exculpatory evidence, you must prove that either Officers or the prosecution maliciously destroyed or lost this evidence, which is difficult to prove considering the high standard set by caselaw. Many of these violations are essentially discovery violations. In cases where the State destroys or loses exculpatory evidence during a case, one should preserve the matter for appeal by filing a motion to either dismiss the case or requesting a mistrial be granted on the grounds of failing to preserve Brady Evidence. But the underlying truth is unless the evidence is of such a nature that it can undoubtedly, no questions ask, and no strings attached exonerate you or raise serious doubts as to your guilt or innocence; most trial judges will perhaps declare a mistrial but will rarely ever dismiss the case. Again, it will always depend on how relevant the evidence is to your defense.

I once heard someone say the Rules of Evidence is the single most important source of legal material a defendant can take to trial. A sentiment I attest to 100%, but not for reasons he had in mind. I say this because physical evidence itself is no longer the main determining factor jurors utilize to determine guilt or innocence. For example, throughout the criminal justice system, it is all too common for juries to return guilty verdicts for charges of armed robbery without the prosecution ever needing to produce the physical weapon allegedly used into evidence. Defendants are subject to convictions for drug trafficking offenses without prosecutors needing to produce actual drugs into evidence. It is common to see convictions for murder without the prosecution ever having to produce a murder weapon. It is also typical for juries to return guilty verdicts for rape without the prosecution needing to produce not even a single strand of DNA evidence.

This is not to imply that every defendant is innocent but more so to demonstrate how unessential physical evidence is becoming. In theory, physical evidence serves to make a particular fact more probable than it would be without it. There was once a time that physical evidence was the primary standard in determining guilt, but this likely changed in the wake of the infamous case that brought to bear, "If the glove doesn't fit, you must acquit." It is now common for prosecutors to bombard defendants with a mountain of physical evidence in hopes of it overwhelming defendants into mismanaging their defense. In response to this bombarding, many defendants play right into the prosecutor's hand by preoccupying themselves solely with discrediting all this physical evidence. This tactic serves to distract defendants from the greater battle, which is the battle of the circumstantial narrative. Physical evidence alone will never convict you without an accompanying theory of facts. The prosecution's true means of attack is through oral testimony from witnesses thereby creating a circumstantial narrative. This serves to frame their theory of the case, which correlates with the circumstantial elements of the offense. The prosecution's theory will always essentially be the elements of a charge presented in narrative form. Thus, you will never hear a prosecutor argue, "I can prove the defendant physically committed the crime, I just don't know how it was committed." The prosecution's case will always be a theory of facts that complement the evidence.

Oral testimony from victims, police officers, medical professionals, eyewitnesses, lay witnesses, expert witnesses, and character witnesses all provide the true foundation prosecutors use to frame theories in a way jurors can conceive. Physical evidence is incapable of speaking, expressing, or conveying the ideas or emotions jurors most heavily rely on to make determinations. For this reason, victimless crimes are the most difficult to prosecute and least likely to be taken to trial. In trials, jurors often have the responsibility of piecing together incomplete stories from both the prosecution and the defense. This impossible task prompts jurors to rely mostly on the type of evidence they can most readily identify with, which are human beings. Understanding this dynamic, prosecutors will generally subpoena as many witnesses as possible. The only means for defendants to offset this tactic is to put together a string of witnesses that will alternatively acknowledge the theory you are presenting as a defense. This will take creativity and resources because in certain situations, there just may not be any witnesses to subpoena. And even in situations where there are witnesses, collecting and readying them for trial can be extremely challenging to say the least.

None of this is to insinuate that defendants should not take evidence seriously, whether it is physical, oral or any other form of evidence. In this situation, you must attempt to defend against any evidence there is against you, no matter how trivial it may appear. But like everything in life, there is a proper way this must be carried out. And this proper way is called a "Suppression hearing". Suppression Hearings are like a defense mechanism to defendants in that you can use them to render evidence obsolete. There are many people under the assumption that Suppression hearings can only be sought for particular types of evidence when this is not the case. There is no legal authority prohibiting defendants from seeking to suppress any particular type of evidence. In fact, the United States Supreme Courts established that *"the entire purpose of a pretrial suppression hearing is to ensure that the accused will not be unfairly convicted by contaminated evidence."* You can attempt to suppress any evidence. And if you utilize your Five felony Weaponry to construct a sound argument as to how a particular piece of evidence in your case is contaminated, there is a possibility the court may agree and suppress that evidence preventing it from being introduced during the trial. The way to initiate a suppression hearing is like anything else in this process, you must motion the Court. (See example Suppression **Motion pg. 269**) By filing a Motion to suppress elaborating your arguments and clarifying how your Constitutional rights have or will be violated by this evidence, the court will decide whether to grant you an evidentiary hearing. Now the kicker is that there is no clearly established Federal caselaw mandating that the court must grant you this hearing. Caselaw establishes that suppression hearings are preferable but not absolute. There is a possibility your request for a hearing could be denied. But the more effectively you litigate the arguments in your motion, the more likely the judge is to grant this hearing out of nothing more but due diligence. If this hearing is granted the United States Supreme Court in <u>United States v. Raddatz,</u> 447 U.S. 667, has held that *"The process due at a suppression hearing may be less demanding and elaborate than the protections accorded a defendant at the trial itself."* This means the suppression hearing will provide only your most basic rights, such as a right to be heard and a right to confront and cross-examine any witnesses. At this hearing, you will have a chance to argue why the evidence should be suppressed and subpoena and cross-examine witnesses as to the evidence. The witnesses will generally be those who were in direct contact with the evidence you are attempting to suppress, which is typically police officers. But there is great benefit in this hearing if used wisely because not only does cross examining police officers provide you the prospect of suppressing the evidence against you, but it also provides you the opportunity to question officers in such a way that they compromise the established narrative of the case, something that will be discussed in later chapters.

12

"ARE YOU NOT ENTERTAINED?

"ISNT THIS WHY YOU ARE HERE!"

Criminal trials are in essence a sham of what the founders of the Federal Constitution originally constructed them to be. Much like the battles that took place in the movie Gladiator, trials are now a show of presentation, performance, and art. When jurors enter a jury box, this entire process conditions them to anticipate a show. After the show, they make their decisions based on which party delivers the better performance, as the better performance will usually equate to the more conceivable theory of facts. To give you an idea of how your jury will approach the theory of the case, you must first understand that this legal process relegates the juror role to one of experience rather than fact-finding. The very structure of the jury trial encourages juries to decide guilt or innocence based on which set of facts they find most conceivable. Which is unreasonable, this is like polling a group of individuals leaving a movie theater on how conceivable the plot was. Regardless of whether the plot was conceivable or not, this still does not address the most important aspect, which is if the plot was factually true. Similarly, the criminal justice system is leading juries to deliberate on how conceivable guilt is rather than how certain they are in their ascertainment of the facts, which are two different questions. Though the two may sound the same, there is a difference. The process of being certain of a conclusion after ascertaining the facts entails actively constructing and deconstructing doubt in a way that brings about one's certainty. Throughout the trial, jurors do not have the luxury to engage in any doubt they have. If jurors are not given any opportunity to employ a given doubt they have, how can it be determined they are reaching a verdict beyond a reasonable doubt? One might presume that jurors can do this during deliberations but at this point of the trial all means of persuasion have concluded, so any process of doubt is inoperable. It is my opinion that jurors should have an opportunity to exercise doubt in the form of presenting specific questions to any party during a trial, and not just during the deliberation phase. In the absence of such, jurors are not given an opportunity to 'reasonably doubt.' However, this is just me venting my opinion. Furthermore, the court never provides juries with a clear-cut definition of what "beyond a reasonable doubt" means. Caselaw admonishes judges against defining it and limits when they even attempt to. So not only are juries ignorant as to how to utilize reasonable doubt, but oftentimes they have no idea what it means to begin with.

As mentioned, this process systematically conveys to jurors the idea that they should choose the theory they can most readily conceive of through their own subjective perspective rather than utilizing the process of fact-finding. Anyone who has ever witnessed a trial would notice much of the prosecution's strategy is not proving the truth but framing what I call the Circumstantial Theory[30]. And what makes Circumstantial Theory so critical is that it directly correlates with the most important component of the trial, which are the jury instructions.

In my opinion, in our criminal justice system, jury instructions in criminal cases are fashioned in such a way that puts defendants at a disadvantage from the start due to a legal ideate I call circumstantial elements. This **idea of Circumstantial elements** [31] entails that the criminal elements comprised in jury instructions are constructed in such a way to subtly impress upon jurors a prosecution-oriented theory of facts which will automatically infer guilt. Additionally, what makes these circumstantial elements so prejudicial is they will always leverage the prosecution's theory more so than the actual evidence against the defendant. In trials, there is a difference between the theory the prosecution presents and the actual evidence. A theory is just the purported narrative of the crime, while the evidence serves to make the theory more tangible and thus more or less believable. The problem is that the elements of jury instructions place the jury's focus on the prosecution's theory by default. Moreover, the nature of guilt-oriented jury instructions sensationalizes the circumstantial theory of a case above that of the physical evidence. Furthermore, circumstantial elements, which make up jury instructions are prejudicially one-sided and will always correlate with the prosecutor's sole interest in a case, which is a conviction. Circumstantial elements unduly pervade the fact-finding process, something caselaw adamantly insists to be an exclusive function of the jury. The example on the next page is layout of what these guilt-oriented instructions will look like to the jury:

You will find the Defendant guilty of First-Degree Assault under this Instruction if, and only if, you believe from the evidence beyond a reasonable doubt all of the following:

> A. That in this county on or about July 9th, 2016, and before the finding of the indictment herein, the defendant caused serious physical injury to Officer Ronald Caffee by unlawfully fleeing from police apprehension.
>
> AND
>
> B. That in so doing, the Defendant was engaging in conduct which created grave risk of death to another and thereby injured Officer Ronald Caffee under circumstances manifesting extreme indifference to the value of human life.
>
> AND
>
> C. (1) That the Defendant was aware of and consciously disregarded a substantial and unjustifiable risk that his conduct would result in Officer Ronald Caffee's serious physical injury, and that his disregard of that risk constituted a gross deviation from the standard of conduct that a person would have observed in the same situation.

The above jury instruction does three things that prejudicially undermine defendants,

1). It makes 'reasonable doubt' an instrument of deliberation rather than an element of guilt the Constitution created it to be thus rendering it obsolete.

2). It minimizes the role that evidence plays in establishing guilt or innocence,

3). It advertently emphasizes the circumstantial elements or the "prosecution's theory" in a way that is prejudicial to the defendant.

But the problem with elements being inherently descriptive in nature is there is oftentimes an unbridgeable gap when one tries to translate a descriptive scenario into circumstantial fact. Or in other words, the elements that make up offenses on paper tend to diverge from circumstances as they exist in the physical. In some situations, the two may not smoothly overlap which would make it somewhat challenging for juries during deliberations. So as a result, the criminal justice system has enabled prosecutors to frame circumstantial elements in a way that incorporates only the prosecution's theory as seen above. In essence, it can be observed that prosecutors are not subject to the same standard of proof in terms of corroborating the elements of an offense, as compared to the defendant. Because of this, the prosecutor's theory thus becomes the elements of the crime. Which means, prosecutors are not having to convince jurors that a defendant's guilt is based on actions that satisfy certain elements but are rather dictating upon them guilt by repeatedly rehearsing a particular theory that may not encompass the actual elements of the offense. Again, to do this, prosecutors will subpoena countless witnesses to reiterate the same theory repeatedly. This serves to reinforce to the jury the same theory of facts until it unconsciously serves as the standard of guilt. Then, at the close of all of the evidence, prosecutors present closing arguments, which further establishes the same theory jurors have heard echoed repeatedly. By the time jurors get to the deliberation phase, a circumstantial theory has been etched in their minds to such an extent that they presume the standard of guilt to be this theory, which prosecutors have the advantage of incorporating into the jury instructions.

This, in most cases, leads to an almost coerced guilty verdict. This is essentially how in many cases, the facts and evidence become obsolete. The actual truth is something most prosecutors are rarely seeking in trials. Remember, for prosecutors, the truth-seeking process happens during police investigation. Once the trial begins, the only truth they will ever acknowledge is your guilt. One might naively presume the elements of a charge to be a means to the truth, but the elements are only a means to the State's truth. The only time you hear the word "truth" in trial is when the Court questions someone before taking the standby asking: "do you swear to tell the truth". Which begs the question. Why do Courts not also pose this same question to prosecutors?

So just imagine if defendants were to have the same leeway prosecutors have and were not restricted in what evidence they could introduce enabling them to subpoena countless witnesses who retold their theory of facts repeatedly throughout the case. Imagine if defendants were able to provide instructions to the jury that correlated with their theory of the case. Would there be any question as to how defendants would fare in criminal trials then?

There are times when jurors cannot control a particular doubt they have, to the extent of interposing certain questions to the judge in the middle of the trial. In any instance that juries attempt to pose such questions, judges will often make it difficult to get the proper understanding they seek. Ironically, the two legal terms through which judges do respond to questions from juries are through "admonishments" and "instructions". As both words, strip the juror of an inclination to exercise their own discretion. Therefore, you must set the tone by seeking to admonish the jury in ways most conducive to your theory of facts. You must also seek **presumptions** [32] relative to the circumstances of your defense. Keep in mind, there is no set situation for presumptions. Thus, you can attempt to frame them any way you would like. The court will deny many of the presumptions you request because judges are keenly aware of the influence presumptions have on the facts of the case. The more presumptions you can have dictated to a jury, the more you alter the real facts, which can be advantageous depending on your circumstances. Therefore, if you were to ask for five presumptions and receive only one, this would be better than nothing at all. For it is impossible to score if you never shoot the ball.

13

"CONTROLLING THE NARRATIVE"

The Importance of Establishing the Theory

> *"The procedures by which the facts of the case are determined assume an importance fully as great as the validity of the substantive role of law to be applied.*
> Speiser v. Randall. 357 U.S. 513

I once knew someone who would constantly preach how important it was not to allow the State to control the narrative of a case, but what he was alluding to was the narrative of the facts on appeal. The factual narratives that make up appeals are called a Statement of the Case. And while managing the narrative in post-conviction proceedings are also important, managing the narrative of facts during pretrial are even more important. The reason being is the narrative of the facts established in the beginning of a case will ultimately become the theory the prosecution presents during trial. And theories are now the primary means of consideration for juries when rendering verdicts. As a result, the value of evidence on its face has greatly diminished. Every single defendant in the criminal justice system starts in the hole as prosecutors often dictate what I call **Narrative Control** [33]. This 'legal ideate' I call Narrative Control begins initially with police officers first establishing the narrative of the incident in police reports. Police officers make sure that witnesses reestablish this same narrative in criminal complaints. Afterwards, nurses and doctors repeat this same narrative in hospital reports, further prompting any witnesses and victims to echo this same narrative as well. During the grand jury hearings, officers will again testify to this same narrative, followed by your eventual indictment, which classifies your charges in such a way that describes this same narrative. If you have a suppression hearing, officers will again testify to this same narrative at the hearing. Finally, during the trial, prosecutors will then subpoena all of the individuals to testify again in person under oath to this same narrative. The prosecution will then move to introduce all of these complaints, reports and affidavits into the record making them accessible for the jury to read. By the time the jury deliberates, the prosecution will have exposed them to a particular narrative enough times that they know it like the back of their own hands. This system has conditioned prosecutors to establish the narrative in their favor going into trial, which is why judges preemptively limit any evidence you introduce that could even potentially weigh unfavorably against the narrative the State establishes. The key to understanding how to utilize evidence advantageously in a case lies in understanding that all evidence is merely a medium you must use to establish your own circumstantial theory. The criminal justice system parades reasonable doubt as if it is a defendant's best friend, but this standard does not apply to evidence on its face. In trial, doubts only apply to natural events and circumstances, not physical evidence. There is no doubt one can apply to a gun on its face. Doubt can only apply to an individual using that gun at a particular place and time. A jury will never acquit you of murder merely because you pass a polygraph test, or because there is no gunshot residue substantiating that you never fired a weapon. The same way a jury does not have to acquit you of rape simply because there exists no physical DNA evidence. Doubt is a conception, so jurors need something conceptual to apply it to; for this reason, they need a theory. Unless you can first present a theory jurors can conceive of, reasonable doubt will do you no good. As it stands, most juries will rarely acquit defendants because the State fails to convince or rather entertain them. The cases jurors do acquit defendants of will most likely be in situations that defendants have provided an alternate theory in which to rival the prosecutions. The evidence you present must always correlate with your theory of facts, your defense, and your innocence. This means you should never present evidence merely to contradict the prosecutor's evidence without a supporting theory. Many fall headlong into this detrimental trap. You must keep in mind jurors are human beings, not robots. If I were on trial for a charge of infidelity and the prosecution had a star witness testify that, they saw me at a restaurant wearing a white, button up shirt conversing with a woman who was not my wife. How pointless would it be for me to subpoena my own witness merely to testify that I was at the restaurant, but I was not eating dinner, or that I was wearing a black button-up shirt rather than a white one? Presenting such evidence would not prove my innocence. This is an example of using evidence to contradict another form of evidence with no other purpose other than contradiction. This strategy could never provoke reasonable doubt because it does not provide a theory to support my innocence. On the other hand, if I were to subpoena my own witness to testify to seeing me wear a white, bottom-up shirt, because I work at that restaurant as a waiter, which would further explain that I was conversing with the woman due to me taking her order. This defense would further provide reasonable doubt as to the charge of infidelity because it provides evidence along with a conceivable theory corroborating my innocence. This example should also tell us that guilt is almost a given when your defense to an accusation is merely to poke holes in the accuser's theory with no theory to offer of your own.

You should always provide a plausible theory to refute the prosecution. The evidence you present at trial should be purposeful. In this context, Denzel Washington was off base in the movie Training Day when he said, "It's not what you know, it's what you can prove!" For the sake of this book, one can therefore say, *it is not what you can prove, but what a jury will conceivably entertain!* So let any evidence you present in a trial serve to enforce your theory, rather than having your theory try to support your evidence. Because evidence alone will rarely prove anything, unless you are just undeniably innocent, and even then, one should still have some type of theory to invalidate the prosecution's case otherwise one could easily find himself or herself a victim of a false conviction.

In life, the facts are permanent and unsusceptible to change. However, the criminal justice system is like an alternate universe where facts are very much like taxes by way of being susceptible to manipulation, but only if you have the necessary resources. This became apparent in the nationally televised case of Trayvon Martin, where in Florida, a White/Hispanic man shot and killed an unarmed African American teen walking home from school. Now in this situation, there were three theoretical facts that were obvious to the public as well as to the parents of Trayvon Martin, which were, 1). The man, who is not a law enforcement officer, armed with a deadly weapon, sought out and began harassing their son because of the color of his skin. 2). that this man then initiated an altercation by attempting to detain their son against his will, and 3). This man had premeditated desire to shoot and kill an African American in a way he thought would be justified. At trial, this man had the resources to influence the facts in his favor as well as add 2 additional facts the jury had to consider. These facts were, 1). That he was merely a concerned neighborhood lookout guard, who, 2). Confronted who he thought to be a burglar. 3). that his actions were not racially motivated. 4). Established Trayvon Martin as the aggressor which 5). Invoked his no duty to retreat right of self-defense.

Now to the many individuals that identify with Trayvon Martin and his parents, the circumstantial theory of this man's defense were implausible to the extent of being laughable. On the other hand, those who did not identify with Trayvon Martin and who were looking for any theory under the sun that would justify this man's actions, were provided with that opportunity. Ultimately, the jury in Trayvon Martin's case acquits this man not because of some brilliant trial strategy he and his attorney put forth, but more so because the jurors in that case were much more ready to entertain any theory which justified this individual killing an African American adolescent, they unconsciously deemed to be a threat to society. As apparent as race seemed to be in the case, the jurors naively convinced themselves that it played no factor in this man's actions. Like many Americans, the jury could not help but perceive this man as an imprudent protector they cannot do without in society, rather than the cold-blooded killer many in the African American community knew him to be. This demonstrates that establishing your circumstantial theory takes nothing more than a perfect storm of the judge acknowledging your theory, as well as the jury inclining to your theory of facts aside from the prosecutors. Which to be honest, rarely happens for individuals who happen to look like Trayvon Martin.

In <u>Crane v. Ky.</u>, 476 U.S. 683, it can also be demonstrated how prosecutors and law enforcement can dictate the facts of the case. *In this case, a 16-year-old youth, was arrested for a holdup and purportedly confessed to an unrelated shooting of a liquor store clerk and was indicted for Murder. The 16-year-old moved to suppress the confession arguing that it was impermissibly coerced. At the ensuing hearing before a Kentucky State Court, he testified that he had been detained in a windowless room for a protracted period, that he had been surrounded by as many as six police officers during the interrogation, that he had repeatedly requested and been denied permission to telephone his mother and that he had been badgered into making a false confession. In spite of the 16 year old's confession being rife with inconsistences such as the 16 year old telling the police the crime was committed during daylight hours and that he had stolen a sum of money from the cash register but evidence showed that the crime was actually committed at 10:10pm at night and that no money at all was missing from the store, the prosecutor yet moved to prevent the attorney for the 16 year old from introducing any testimony bearing on the circumstances under which the confession was obtained. With no surprise,* the Judge in the 16-year old's case rules in the prosecutions favor ordering that the 16-year old's attorney would not be permitted *to "develop in front of the jury" any evidence about the duration of the interrogation or the individuals who were in attendance.* This is an instance of Narrative Control as the judge prevents the defense from disturbing the prosecution's narrative.

This case also shows you the true nature of many prosecutors. Rather than presenting an accurate and truthful theory of facts from which a jury can determine what happened for themselves, the prosecutor opts to construct a circumstantial theory that would only lead to the jury convicting the 16-year-old without all of the necessary information, even if it amounted to wrongful imprisonment of the teenager. Prosecutors in the criminal justice system are notorious for manipulating a particular theory to serve their interest. As the criminal justice system understands the impact these theories have on juries, they have enabled prosecutors to utilize not just a single theory to convict defendants, but also alternate theories to do such. An alternative theory is a legal concept approved by caselaw, which essentially allows prosecutors to tell juries, "This is exactly how the defendant committed this crime, but if you by chance find the defendant is not guilty of committing it this way, then here is an alternative scenario to use to find him guilty." Now, in what alternate universe is this fair? The concept of fairness entails a standard that applies to everyone equally. In trial, if prosecutors can utilize alternate theories of guilt, then why shouldn't defendants use alternate theories of innocence? The answer is because it would be absurd. How absurd would the defendant look arguing to the jury, "I didn't do it because I was sleep when the crime happened, but if you don't happen to believe I was sleep, you may also believe me when I tell you, I didn't do it because I was at work when the crime happened." How ridiculous would this be? For this reason, defendants cannot present alternative defenses, while prosecutors can unfairly manipulate and alter their theory of the case, in any way that brings about a conviction. The only way for you to even attempt to limit how prosecutors present their theory of facts is by filing a Motion for Bill of Particulars [34] during the early pretrial stages of the case. The Courts have set out that:

> *"The purpose of a Bill of Particulars is to give a defendant key factual information not contained in the indictment, so as to enable him or her to prepare a defense and avoid surprise at trial."* <u>United States V. Page,</u> 575 F. Asp's 641, 643 (6th Cir. 2014): *"The three purposes of a Bill of Particulars are: to inform the defendants of the nature of the charge against him with sufficient precision to enable him to prepare for trial, to avoid or minimize the danger of surprise at the time of trial, and enable him to plead his acquittal or conviction in bar of another prosecution for the same offense when the indictment itself is too vague and indefinite for such purposes."* <u>United States v. Birmley,</u> 529 F. 2d 103, 108 (6th Cir. 1976)

In a request for Bill of particulars, defendants can pose certain questions to the prosecution in a way that compels them to detail the fundamentals of their theory of the case. To some degree, this limits how the prosecution presents its case because it would prohibit them from deviating outside of anything they themselves establish in the Bill of Particulars. A Bill of Particular essentially nails the prosecution down to a particular set of facts rather than allowing them the opportunity to develop the facts throughout the case. However, because this could potentially help defendants, judges will rarely grant these requests. Nonetheless, defendants should still attempt to request them.

Just as prosecutors have various means of molding the theory in a case; defendants also have subtle means of doing so. There are two fundamental means through which defendants can attempt to shape the theory of the facts. The first is by filing pretrial motions to exclude or bar certain evidence; like what the prosecution did in Crane v. Ky. However, most judges are keenly opposing to defendants altering the theory of the facts in anyway, so the only chance you stand of compelling the judge to grant the request is by articulating how such evidence may somehow prejudice your constitutional right to a fair trial protected by 6th and 14 Amendment. You should file this motion asking the court to exclude this evidence by arguing how it violates which state and Federal rights, while also using as much caselaw as possible to support your argument.

The second and perhaps most important means of molding the theory of facts in a case are through presumptive instructions. The purpose of presumptive instructions is to give the jury a clear and concise way to apply certain factors to the facts when deciding a verdict in trial. But in all honesty, presumptive instructions[35] encompass so much more. When rendering a verdict, the legal process requires juries to replace their common sense with what is in the instructions. What this means is before you can succeed in winning the belief of the jury, you must first win the instructions to which their hearts are subject. As mentioned earlier, the most debilitating thing about instructions is they provide juries with the elements of the crime in such a way that renders defendants guilty by default. In other words, the elements are always guilt oriented. We see this with the instructions below,

> *"You will find the defendant guilty of constructive possession of a firearm, if on the day of May 13, the defendant was (1) aware or knew of the firearms*

> *presence and (2) had the ability and intent to later exercise dominion and control over the firearm."*

To juries, the guilt made inherent in these circumstantial elements is easily conceivable, especially when a defendant already fits a description that conforms to a preconceived prejudice they may have. At this point, what leeway do jurors have to entertain any doubt as to these facts? Where does a defendant's theory of facts fit into this instruction? In trials, the only law the jury may apply to the case is what the instructions provide. Many defendants are oblivious to the reality that it is the responsibility of both defendants and prosecutors to participate in the drafting of the jury instructions. In most cases, judges will reject all proposed jury instructions by defendants. Nonetheless, participating in creating one's instructions remains something you must attempt as conveyed in <u>Hana Fin. V. Hana Bank,</u> 574 U.S. 418. wherein it was held,

> *"And insofar as petition is concerned that a jury may improperly apply the relevant legal standard, the solution is to craft careful jury instructions that*

make that standard clear."

The sooner it truly dawns on you that you have a right to participate in drafting your own jury instructions, the sooner you will realize how creative you can be in making these instructions. Again, getting both the prosecutor and judge to agree to what you have proposed is an entirely different battle, but even if they do not accept your instructions in entirety, this will start the bargaining process in a way all sides would have to come to a compromise. By virtue of how important it is to articulate to the jury the elements of the charge, there is limit to how creative you can be in framing the narrative. The standard for creating your own jury instructions is that you must always include every element of the charge for a jury to consider, but the benefit of you creating your own instructions allows you to create your own circumstantial elements in a way that reasonable doubt is not obsolete. My advice would be to try to present your instructions in a way that is innocence oriented, which would look something like the following:

You will find the Defendant "NOT" guilty of First-Degree Assault under this Instruction if, and only if:

C. If you have a Reasonable Certainty that,

D. In this county on or about July 9th, 2016, and before the finding of the indictment herein, he unintentionally and unknowingly caused serious physical injury to Officer Ronald Caffee by unlawfully fleeing from police apprehension.

AND

E. because the Defendant did so unintentionally and unaware, the Defendant's conduct cannot be considered to have created a grave risk of death to another and thereby injured Officer Ronald Caffee under circumstances manifesting extreme indifference to the value of human life.

AND

F. Because the Defendant was consciously unaware, he cannot be said to have consciously disregarded a substantial and unjustifiable risk that his conduct would result in Officer Ronald Caffee's serious physical injury, and if he didn't disregard that risk consciously, his conduct cannot be deemed a gross deviation from the standard of conduct that a person would have observed in the same situation.

(This example correlates with the instruction used on pg. 112)

The only difference between the typical instruction presented on pg. 112 and this instruction is that one is guilt oriented while the other is what I would call an innocence-oriented instruction [36]. Legally, this type of instruction is only an example to make a point but, it is more consistent with fairness. Such an instruction would level the playing field for defendants, so the chance of a judge and the prosecution agreeing to such an instruction is slim to none. Nevertheless, in many states, this is a constitutionally sufficient instruction by way of it providing a jury every element needed to convict a defendant of first-Degree Assault but also those needed to acquit him. Therefore, if you were to customize your instruction to suit your respective State law it should apply to you as well. Obviously, such an instruction comes off a little leading, but no less leading than the typical instructions that are guilt oriented and since this criminal justice system propagates the idea that defendants are presumed innocent until proven guilty, it would make more sense that juries have innocence-oriented instructions rather than guilty. As mentioned before, most Courts may not accept this type of instruction, but this should show you what type of mentality you must have as you go into constructing your jury instructions. Additionally, it is through instructions that defendants can request that presumptive instructions be given, and these can be used very shrewdly. A presumptive instruction is an additional means of dictating the facts. The difference between these and admonishments is presumptive instructions are what juries utilize during jury deliberations to apply the law, while admonishments are what jurors utilize to apply the facts. Presumptions are in essence, manufactured facts jurors must factor into their deliberation. The federal courts define these presumptive presumptions as assumptions of fact that the law requires to be made from another fact or group of facts found or otherwise established in the action or proceeding. Presumptions can change the facts of the case in a way that helps the defense, something that rarely happens in criminal cases. Therefore, with a creative defense, support from the Court, and the right jury it is possible to exploit presumptions in a way that complements your theory of facts. Nevertheless, one must not get too discouraged if the Judge rejects such instructions or presumptions, for this is the nature of the criminal justice system.

14

"THE STAGES OF BATTLE"

The Legal Process

(A). District Court

Anybody who has ever been through the criminal justice system will vividly remember the first experience like a nightmare that cannot be forgotten. The ride in the back of the police car, the interrogation by police, the first-time walking into a county jail, or the first-time walking into a courtroom shackled and restrained. All of these experiences remain etched in one's memory because of how raw and strange the experience. The onset of one's arrest seems like the beginning of a completely new state of existence, one of misery, confusion, shame, anxiety, and dreadfulness. During this time, there is a lot of moving parts that seem confusing and arbitrary. I believe it would be helpful to provide a brief step-by-step outline of what to expect during this process. My hope is to provide a measure of consolation during this time of distress. This step- by-step illustration may include some of what I have previously mentioned but it is primarily for those who will experience the criminal justice experience from inside of the belly. This includes those who are accused serious felony offense(s) such as Murder, Attempted Murder, Armed Robbery, Assault or Battery, Burglary, Possession of Firearms, or serious Trafficking offenses. Such individuals will normally have bail set in a range of $50,000 to $100,000 or more. These high bonds are to ensure defendants will likely have to fight their indictment under adverse conditions in jail, which ultimately benefits prosecutors.

    The beginning of this experience starts when you

are booked into the county jail. In every jail, there is usually a book-in section of the jail reserved for those charged with minor and low-level criminal offenses. The Courts usually release these individuals either on their 'own recognizance' or on bail. You will usually see a lot of drunks, prostitutes, drug addicts, the homeless and those whose conduct was so disorderly it led to having to spend the night in jail. One might spend roughly two or three days here before one's initial appearance before a judge. Depending on the state, this court may be called the district court or the magistrate. These district or magistrate judges will generally hear minor misdemeanor offenses, family court, and traffic offenses. Etc.

Now, this first and initial arraignment in the district court means little to nothing. At this arraignment, a judge will provide you with notice of the charges against you, an opportunity to plead guilty or not guilty and issue you a bond. Because your charges are serious felony offenses, this first judge understands your case is out of their jurisdiction and will not give sincere consideration to your release. However, both the charges and the bond you will likely receive at this stage may be the lowest they will ever be because at this point the facts and evidence against you are still in dispute. If your bail is set at something you by chance can make, you should immediately make a bond because more than likely both your bail and your charges will increase as the process proceeds forward.

The most significant aspect for defendants during this preliminary stage is that during this phase the court must determine if enough probable cause exists for the case to proceed any further. It is your first weaponry, the Fourth Amendment providing you a right to a probable cause/preliminary hearing.[37] Meaning, this determination of probable cause is necessary otherwise; your detainment is unlawful pursuant to the United States Constitution. The Fourth Amendment provides that all defendants in custody have an absolute right to probable cause hearings no matter what State you occupy. The United States Supreme Court supports this in holding:

> *"Whatever procedure a State may adopt, it must provide a fair and reliable determination of probable cause as a condition for any significant pretrial restraint of liberty, and this determination must be by a judicial officer either before or promptly after arrest."* <u>Gerstein v. Pugh</u>... /20 US 103

However, the standard the State must prove at these hearings is bare minimum to say the least. <u>Bringer v. United States,</u> 338 U.S., at 174-175 holds that,

> *"In dealing with probable cause, however, as the very name implies, we deal with probabilities. These are not technical; they are the factual and practical consideration of everyday life on which reasonable and prudent men, not legal technicians, act. The standard of proof is accordingly correlative to what must be proved."*

Or to be even more blunt <u>Gerstein v. Pugh</u> has held,

> *probable cause to believe the suspect has committed a crime, traditionally has been decided by a magistrate in a non-adversary proceeding on hearsay and written testimony, and the (United States Supreme Court) has approved these informal modes of proof.*

This means that unless you're just flat-out innocent of the accusations, you will typically not prevail in these hearings because the standard of proof the State must meet for probable cause is so low. On the flip side, probable cause hearings could potentially help to complement your defense as evidence from such hearings can sometimes be used to establish and build your circumstantial theory at trial as many states allow testimonial evidence from probable cause hearings to be introduced during the trial. This could possibly provide you an opportunity to jump-start your trial strategy by presenting evidence or subpoenaing witnesses to offer testimony that potentially establishes a set of facts to your favor. For example, if a witness identifies you as the perpetrator by a particular description and you subpoena another witness to dispute the description, this sets the tone for your defense going forward. If you remember, just earlier I told you such a strategy is illogical during trials, but when it comes to probable cause hearings, such evidence goes to establishing your theory. The probable cause hearing can also be a means to pin down the facts of the case. This could be vital as it is common for prosecutors to often expand the facts of the case to the extent of even enhancing or adding more charges. Probable cause hearings are something many defendants are not aware of, because many attorneys waive these hearings on their behalf without notifying them. The way to prevent this is to tell the judge during your initial arraignment that you do not wish to waive your probable cause hearing. If you manage to establish this at your initial arraignment hearing, you have evidence on the record proving you invoked your right to this hearing, so your attorney cannot waive it on your behalf. In all States but Alabama, caselaw establishes probable cause hearings are not a critical stage of the proceedings, so defendants are not entitled to basic due process rights during these hearings. These hearings will typically be informal, consisting only of testimony from material witnesses. If by chance, the court denies you a probable cause hearing or if your attorney waives it on your behalf, this becomes a claim you possibly can utilize on appeal. The United States Supreme Court holds in Manuel v. City of Juliet, 580 U.S.357(2017):

> "The Fourth Amendment is tailored

explicit for the criminal justice system, and it always has been thought to define the appropriate process for seizures of persons in criminal cases, including the detention of suspects pending trial. That Amendment, standing alone, guarantees a fair and reliable determination of probable cause as a condition of any significant pretrial restraint. Accordingly, those detained prior to trials without such a finding an appeal to the Fourth Amendment protection against unfounded invasions of liberty."

After the probable cause hearing, the judge will then decide if probable cause exists and if so, will then dismiss your case from the lower court so it could then be sent to the grand jury to determine if you'll be indicted by the higher, felony court.

(B). GRAND JURY PROCEEDINGS

Judicial precedent recognizes the Grand jury's singular role in finding probable cause necessary to initiate a prosecution for a serious crime. An indictment fair upon its face and returned by a properly constituted grand jury conclusively determines the existence of probable cause to believe the defendant perpetrated the offense alleged. And conclusively means, case in and case out, just that. There is no authority for looking into and revising the judgment of the grand jury upon the evidence, for the purpose of determining whether or not the finding was founded upon sufficient proof to the contrary, the whole history of the grand jury institution demonstrates that a challenge to the reliability or competence of the evidence supporting a grand jury's. finding of probable cause will not be heard. The grand jury gets to say, without any review, oversight, or second guessing, whether probable cause exists to think that a person committed a crime.

~Kagan, J., Joined by Scalia, Kennedy, Thomas, Ginsburg and Alita, JJ.

The United States Supreme Court

Do not let the term grand jury confuse you. These are not the same jurors during trial that determines if you're guilty or not guilty. These are the jurors responsible for initiating the whole process by deciding whether to issue a true bill, or in other words an indictment. At first blush, you might look at the grand jury's issuing of an indictment as a negative but grand jury indictments are not wholly suggestive of guilt or innocence. Indictments from grand juries are routine in most cases, so this should tell you not to put too much stock when the grand jury returns an indictment. As mentioned in the previous chapter, probable cause is the standard for issuing an indictment, which is an unbelievably low standard to prove. This standard of probable cause is merely to determine if enough evidence exists for detaining a person to stand trial. It does not necessarily indicate guilt. Therefore, do not be discouraged or intimidated by your indictment.

In most states defendants cannot be present during these grand jury proceedings. There has always been a lot of obscurity about the grand jury process, but this obscurity is purposeful. Caselaw establishes that " *and jury secrecy is an integral part of the criminal justice system"* and that *"the grand jury as a public institution serving the community might suffer if those testifying today knew that the secrecy of their testimony would be lifted tomorrow. "* For this reason, retrieving information about grand jury hearings other than the hearing transcripts can be difficult. Those present at these hearings will normally be the judge, prosecutor and the 12 jurors the court clerk selects from a random jury pool. Much like a jury trial, the jury of 12 will vote on a jury foreman who directs the process. One must keep in mind many of the random individuals in the jury pool are likely to be conservatives who have no idea about the true nature of the criminal justice system. These individuals are more likely to issue an indictment in haste, just to make sure they're not letting the guilty off the hook. What is odd is, in many States there is no judge in these proceedings, and it is the prosecutor who serves in the role as the overseer of these proceedings conveying to the jury their responsibilities while also serving in the adversarial role against defendants. How the courts have come to conclude that prosecutors could serve both roles and it does not prejudice the defendant is unfathomable. Prosecutors are literally walking into grand jury proceedings presenting just accusatory statements from arresting officers and securing indictments. In essence, this process could not be more prejudicial to a defendant because it provides the State with an adversarial advantage before the war even begins. In many states, attorneys can present evidence on their client's behalf but in many cases, attorneys will choose not to do so. In some cases, insisting your attorney mount some type of defense on your behalf during the grand jury proceedings is probably in your best interest. With that in mind, it's also important for you to consider the grand jury's decision not to indict, may not automatically preclude a subsequent indictment in the future.

(C). **PRE-TRIAL**

After the Grand jury process and after being indicted, this brings you to what most states call the Circuit Court or the Superior Court. This process begins with you again being arraigned at another arraignment hearing. Like all arraignment hearings, a Circuit judge will again provide notice of the charges against you, provide you a chance to enter a plea, and issue you another bond, sometimes much higher than the first. During this arraignment hearing, you may notice you also have a new prosecutor, so don't be surprised if this prosecutor enhances your charges. It is normal for prosecutors to do this because by then the prosecutors have now examined all of the evidence against you and made their decision on what charges are most appropriate. In fact, prosecutors have the discretion to indict a defendant on enhanced or additional charges at any point before the trial. During pretrial it's not out of the realm of possibility that you go to court, only to realize you have another indictment with more charges against you. If the new prosecutor adds more charges to the indictment, you should always object on the grounds of vindictiveness, prosecutor misconduct and malicious prosecution if nothing more to preserve these issues for appeal. Courts will usually deny this claim by defendants, but this is merely to preserve this issue on the record for appeal.

At this point, there will always be this idea that any little defect, technicality, or error one finds in the indictment is a means to getting the entire case dismissed. But this is how it works in movies; this is not reality. As it stands, the Courts are gradually making it more difficult to get one's case dismissed in the pretrial stages of a case. **Which is not to say it is impossible,** but just that it is becoming increasingly difficult. Minor typos, defects, and errors you find in your discovery are typically not enough to quash an indictment. Caselaw establishes:

> *"An indictment must allege each and every essential element of the charges offense in order to pass constitutional muster." United States v. Shelton, 937 F. 2d at 142. However, the Court must also be mindful that "the law does not compel a ritual of words," and that the validity of an indictment depends on practical, not technical, considerations. United States v. Ratcliff, 488 F/ 3d 639, 643 (5th Cir. 2007)*

At the first pretrial hearing, it is typical for judges to schedule a trial date. In most cases, this is just pretrial decorum and is not the date you will go to trial. In many instances, this can inadvertently serve as a scare tactic, as many defendants hear this date and start panicking with the impression the State is taking them to trial. This anxiety may prompt them to take a less favorable plea bargain out of haste. Keep in mind, despite these trial dates, judges understand pretrial hearings are indispensable to both the rights of defendants and prosecutors. They understand these pretrial hearings are necessary to ensure a fair trial. The last thing any judge wants is for a higher court to scold them for some violation that occurs in their courtroom. Therefore, it is normal for the courts to cycle through 4 or 5 trial dates aware that none of the dates will be the trial dates.

In all gangster movies, whenever there is an intense shooting scene about to take place, there is always a scene with a group of individuals studiously cleaning, loading, and checking their arsenal of weapons in preparation for what looks like all-out war. In the context of the criminal justice system, the pre-trial phases of the case serve as that very scene for defendants. The last thing you want to do is go into war ill equipped or to have your weapons malfunction during a battle. For this reason, it is so important to have not just a trial strategy but also a pre-trial strategy. As mentioned in an earlier chapter, a decision whether to go to trial is contingent on how successful your pretrial strategy is. Without an effective pretrial strategy, it is impossible to have a productive trial strategy. When formulating a pretrial strategy, you must objectively delineate which factors will give you the best chance of prevailing at trial. 'The only way to know what provides you the best chance at prevailing at trial is by familiarizing yourself with the elements of each charge against you. For defendants, a proper understanding of these elements provides insight as to what you must do to weaken the prosecutor's ability to prove them. This may include things such as getting a crucial piece of evidence against you ruled inadmissible, convincing a judge to grant you a favorable presumption, or presenting evidence into the record that can discredit your accusers at trial. Developing a pretrial strategy consists of knowing the elements that make up the charges against you. It is so important that defendants memorize by heart the elements of the charges against them. For in this war, these elements are your roadmap.

For those not utilizing the services of a paid

attorney, the pretrial phase should be when you meet the attorney the court appoints to represent you. This usually consists of your attorney coming to visit you at the jail for a face-to-face conference. This is also around the time you should be expecting to receive your discovery from your attorney. As mentioned before, discovery is a record of all of the evidence the State has against you. Most states now provide discovery digitally on compact disc or a flash drive. The prosecution will usually send your discovery to your attorney, who will then forward it to you at the institution where you are housed. The first couple of pretrial hearings will consist of your attorney attempting to get you some form of pretrial release, if possible. However, the more serious your charges are, the less likely judges are to grant you pretrial release. Unless you have a wealthy relative or an associate willing to put up cash or property for your bond, it's best not to stake too much claim in fighting this war on the streets.

For defendants, the pretrial phase of the case is where you should attempt to mold the outcome of the trial in your favor. This happens by doing everything in your power to make sure you receive the fairest trial possible. After fully internalizing the five felony Weaponry (the five Amendments) in a way you understand, one must then consider all of the factors of your case and conceptualize what obstacles even potentially stand to threaten your right to a fair trial. Earlier in the book, I mentioned how the biggest mistake many defendants make is using what they think is fair, right, and just to argue one's case, which works to their ignorance. But once you've developed a proper grasp and understanding of how to exercise your weaponry this allows you to litigate your arguments more effectively. It's been said hindsight is 20-20, but in this situation, it is foresight that is 20-20. In order to effectively advocate for your position, it is advisable to identify a definitive constitutional breach that can be leveraged to your advantage. However, if such a violation is not immediately apparent, it is prudent to analyze the potential for any given issue to develop into a constitutional error by the time of the trial. By developing anticipatory arguments based on this analysis, you can strategically lay the groundwork for a constitutional challenge. When an individual has sufficient skill and a comprehensive understanding of the law, applying this principle will greatly help ones defense. Or, at the very least it may just provide you with more leverage in negotiating the best plea bargain. Therefore, when you are conceiving an idea of what fairness looks like in your case, my advice is to be as creative as possible. Use your heart to discern what seems to be unfair and use caselaw to substantiate and further litigate it to the court. There is no such thing as a perfect trial. Fairness, theoretically speaking, is not a fixed concept but rather something that defendants can stretch along constitutional lines. There are many issues and situations that can happen throughout this process that may infringe upon one's right to a fair trial, but one must first recognize, present, and litigate them in a way that Courts will acknowledge.

If your attorney happens not to agree with your pretrial strategy or with what you deem to be an infringement on your right to a fair trial, you must still know how to convey these arguments to the judge for determination. Because though your attorney may disagree with you about a particular argument, it is you, not your lawyer, who will suffer for failing to preserve them on the record for appeal. The choice is nonetheless yours to make. The Federal Courts have held,

> The Sixth Amendment provides that "[i]n all criminal prosecutions, the accused shall enjoy the right to have the assistance of counsel for his defense." In the jurisprudence concerning the Sixth Amendment, the Supreme Court has explained that this right "does not provide merely that defense shall be made for the accused; ii grants to the accused personally the right to make his defense." Farella V California, 422 US. 806, 819, 95 S. Ct. 2525, 45 L. Ed. 2d 562. See also United States v. Plattner, 330 F. 2d 271, 274, (2d Cir. 1964) (/implicit ....is the right of the accused personally to manage conduct his own defense in a criminal case.") This right encompasses the decision of what defenses a particular defendant wished to advance and other 'fundamental trial decisions." Petrovich v. Leonardo, 229 F. 3d 384, 386-87(2d Cir. 200).

The above language provides you with a basis to override your attorney if you have a reasonable constitutional violation to present to the court. In such a situation, defendants must preserve and present these arguments to the court directly through filing a pro se motion. And if the judge inquires as to why you have chosen to undermine your attorney by filing a motion pro se, one should use the language above to remind the court of what the Supreme Court says about your right to present your own defense through your attorney as set out by the Sixth Amendment. Anytime you file something in your own right, many judges and attorneys will attempt to use that to corner you into self-representation. If this happens and that is not your intention, establish on the record that it is not your intention to represent yourself but rather to preserve the record for appeal. The more familiar you are with your five Felony Weaponry, the more equipped you'll be to defend against such attacks.

15

"THE LAST STAND"

The Trial

1) Voir Dire

In the pre-stages of the trial, the court will randomly draw and select an array of potential jurors that will make up the jury pool. The jury pool will be a group of usually 25-30 random people, constitutionally described as a group of your peers, but rarely will any of these individuals share your cultural, social, or economic background if you are a minority. Which unfortunately, is the determining factor in how juries determine a case, as we all perceive people's character through the prism of how we personally identify with them. If these individuals cannot identify with you socially, the likelihood of them identifying with any type of defense you present will also be problematic. For this reason, defendants have a right to challenge the array of the entire jury pool, but these challenges rarely prevail. This means if one attempts to make such a challenge, the argument and you're reasoning for requesting it must be nothing short of sound.

In some States, it is the trial court that bears the responsibility of examining jurors before trial. But in most States, this process will begin with both your attorney and the prosecution taking turns to address and examine the jury pool. While addressing the jury pool, the goal for both defendants and the prosecution is to ask general questions for purposes of screening for bias. This may include questions such as:

❖ Do any of the jurors personally know either the

defendant or the prosecutor?

- ❖ Do any of the jurors have family that work in law enforcement or any branch of government,
- ❖ Have any of the jurors or their families been victims of the charges being tried, or
- ❖ Do any of the jurors have family incarcerated for the charges at being tried?

Though the main objective for addressing and examining the jury pool is to weed out bias, this opportunity provides you an indirect opportunity to put your finger on the pulse of the jury. Though many of these potential jurors will not participate in the trial, the remaining members left will ultimately be the 12 who hear the case. This rare and limited opportunity for you to identify with these 12 individuals should be a means to establish a favorable first impression. When addressing the jury pool, defendants also can understand the personal views of jurors on key issues relative to one's defense. All of which can be done through the legal ideates I call, **Question instigating**. [38] For example, if the State were to predicate much of their case on the testimony of a drug addict or drug dealer, when addressing the jury pool, the nature of the questions in which to set the stage for your defense should be something along the lines of:

- ❖ How important do you think creditability is in weighing the testimony of a witness?
- ❖ In your opinion, what are some of the reasons that a drug addict or a drug dealer may testify and lie on the stand?

These questions should instigate an inclination to distrust testimony from such witnesses, so during the trial when such witnesses take the stand, these questions will loom in the back of the jury's mind instigating doubt as to their testimony.

With enough artfulness, there are certain questions you can pose that will expose a jury's ideas about innocence and guilt. For example, defendants have a right not to testify on the stand on their own behalf during trials. But there are many jurors who may maintain that if a defendant is innocent, it would only make sense to testify on their own behalf, thereby also inferring that if a defendant does not testify it can only be an indication of guilt. Oftentimes a juror may express this opinion in a roundabout way, but judges will allow such individuals to sit as jurors anyway so long as when asked if they could be impartial and fair, they maintain they could. When or if you can secure such information from jurors, this can be monumental for your defense because such information helps to provide insight as to what it takes to win a particular juror's belief. Remember, all you need is one juror to believe your theory. On the negative side, this also means during this process, jurors are often acknowledging they hold bias and prejudicial beliefs; Yet courts will give the benefit of the doubt to these jurors presuming they can put such biasness aside with little to no proof of such an ability. In some cases, this could be tantamount to trusting the objectivity of Donald Trump to assess the performance of Barak Obama's presidency. How objective do you really trust such an assessment to be? For decades, prosecutors in our criminal justice system have exercised all of these same tactics against defendants. So not only do these tactics provide you with a weapon to utilize for your defense, but they also provide you with the awareness to defend against it when prosecutors use it against you. It is during this process of voir dire that most jurors form their first impression. It is also during this phase that jurors formulate ideas about the charges, the defendant, your lawyer, the prosecutor and whether they're interested in serving on the jury at all. All of which psychologically factor into their contribution to the verdict. This phase serves almost as a campaign for both prosecutors and defendants. Moreover, if you know anything about political campaigns, you know they are momentous events. They are extensive, elaborate and calculated. For this reason, defendants must also develop voir dire strategies coming into this stage of the proceedings. Such strategies should include, firstly, how to best personify yourself in a way jurors can identify with, second, have a list of instigated questions you wish to impress upon the jury, and thirdly, identify the type of jurors that would best complement your defense verses those who will not.

After addressing and examining the jury pool, both you and the prosecutors can then begin challenging/striking, the jurors you would rather not participate in the trial. There are two standard types of challenges through which defendants can eliminate jurors from the jury pool. These challenges are, 1). To challenge (strike) for cause, and 2). Peremptory challenges (peremptory strikes). Both terms are just words that denote removing a juror from the jury pool. Challenges for cause' is a fundamental right of the defendant protected by the Sixth and Fourteenth Amendments of the United States Constitution, which entails that defendants have a constitutional right to a jury of persons who are unbiased and who have at least a basic level of competence. As the defendant, you have an unlimited number of challenges you may use for

Cause. After questioning a juror about a particular matter, it is their reply that provides the basis to determine if they are biased or incompetent. This is why it is so important to frame your questions in a way that prompts these jurors to give an in-depth explanation. The more someone expounds on a matter, the better your chances are at understanding who they are. 'Peremptory Challenges' are different from challenges for Cause in that the United States Constitution does not protect them. The United States Supreme Court has determined,

> *"Because peremptory challenges are within the States province to grant or withhold, the mistaken denial of a state-provided peremptOty challenge does not, without more, violate the Federal Constitution."* <u>Engle v. Isaac,</u> *456 U.S. 107, 121, n 21, 102 S. Ct. 1558, 71 L. Ed. 2d 783 (1982).*

This means you have no federal right to peremptory challenges. Though all States provide these peremptory challenges to defendants, the number of these challenges will vary from state to state due to them being a product of the State constitution rather than the Federal Constitution. These challenges are unique in the sense that they generally provide defendants with the means to strike or remove jurors without any reason whatsoever, but because these challenges are limited, you must make sure to use them wisely.

Just as defendants have a right to these Peremptory Challenges; prosecutors also have a right to them. And if one pays attention, it becomes obvious that prosecutors do not just employ these challenges arbitrarily but rather with a particular strategy in mind. One of the more common and prejudicial strategies of prosecutors is a legal ideate I call Jury Socialization [39]. Jury Socialization is the prosecutions tactic of using social factors against defendants in a way that juries are more likely to return guilty verdicts. One of the many ways that prosecutors employ this tactic is by subtly removing as many African Americans from jury pool as possible. Now, this may seem like "race-baiting" or playing the "race-card", but this is a sad truth.

Regardless of if the defendant is black or white, prosecutors will still usually use their peremptory challenges to remove African Americans regardless of how unbiased and competent they appear to be. The reason for this is perhaps an awareness prosecutors have that African Americans are inclined to be more objective in this process because of the flagrant injustices directed at them in the past even up until the present. Because of this, prosecutors discriminately infer that this makes African Americans less capable of being adequate jurors during trials, and the Courts have done nothing but further empower such tactics. The second component of Jury Socialization is the tactic prosecutors use to exploit the social dynamics of American society. Prosecutors employ this tactic by identifying two key factors when choosing which jurors to sit on the jury: First, which juror will best serve as their guiding current and secondly, which individuals will act as the waves. In this situation, the guiding current symbolizes the individual who will most likely be voted jury foreman and who will set the tone for the rest of the jury during deliberations. The waves are the collective who will likely follow and serve as reinforcement for the guiding current. So, really this tactic by prosecutors is a psychological profiling tactic. Prosecutors understand when these 12 individuals are together in a room alone to deliberate, American socialization takes effect. This is no different from the social dynamic of high school, in that social butterflies thrive and those who are social misfits do not. The only difference is now, the socially superior are not cool kids, now it is the exact opposite; now the socially superior are those individuals everybody picked on in school or those who were not socially active. These individuals now happen to be the very staples of society; these same individuals are now college educated, economically secure and intellectually and emotionally stable. Everyone on the jury will more than likely look to this individual during the deliberation process. The others will most likely be okay with participating and not rocking the boat by following the current wherever it goes. And these are the very social elements that will usually facilitate the outcome of the verdict. This is why prosecutors will aim to strike and remove most African

Americans, Hispanic or Asian men as such individuals serve as threats to uniformity of a jury. In the absence of any other prospects, this leaves the educated, conservative older or middle-aged Caucasian male usually serving as the guiding current. The individuals who serve as the waves will usually be middle aged or older Caucasian females and young adults. Therefore, your strategy for selecting jurors should also consider social dynamics. You must identify whom the prosecution is targeting to serve as the guiding current and move to have them removed from the jury pool. Or, alternatively, you should try to select your own guiding current and waves who will most likely identify with your defense. During Voir Dire, you must utilize Question Instigating [38] to convey to the jury pool how important it is not to just follow the tide, but to think for themselves. Because of the dynamic of our population, most of the jury pool will usually be white.

This has nothing to do with racism; this is just a product of our population. This gives all defendants whether African American, Caucasian, Hispanic, Middle Eastern or Asian the right to ask minorities in the jury pool questions such as, "Because you may end up as the only minority in the jury during deliberations, would you have a problem with disagreeing with the majority if there's something you don't agree with? Or "Are you willing to be the oddball if you disagree with the rest of the jury?" If prosecutors object to such questions, your reasoning should be the racial imbalance of the jury pool.

Once this process is complete, when both the defendant and the prosecutor have exercised their challenges, the remaining jurors will take an oath and be seated, which concludes this stage of the trial.

It's important to keep in mind, the very same jurors you select or fail to remove are not only those who will be deciding the merit of your defense but will also dictate your sentence length if found guilty. This makes it even more important to vet out which jurors that come off as staunch conservatives versus those who appear more liberal. All of this becomes relative depending on the outcome of the verdict. Common sense tells you if you had a choice, you would rather much have the liberal deciding what your punishment will be, as many liberals are those who are against the death penalty. Even in situations that do not involve the death penalty, the difference between these two individuals regarding punishment is usually night and day. Those who are more liberal will be more inclined to mercy and forgiveness, likely rendering punishments that are more lenient and sensible. Conservatives on the other hand, are those who happen to be advocates of harsher sentences and will generally be those, less inclined to mercy and forgiveness. When choosing which jurors to sit or remove, defendants must consider all of these little details because ultimately, all of these things will contribute to the outcome of the trial.

LET'S GET READY TO RUMBLE!

2). *Reading of the Indictment*

At the start of the trial, the Courtroom clerk initiates the process by "giving the defendant into the charge of the jury." This entails the Courts reading out the contents of your indictment before the jury along with informing them of their responsibility in the case.

3). *Opening Statement*

It has been established by the United States Supreme Court,

"The purpose of an opening statement

is to state what evidence will be presented, to make it easier for the jurors to understand what is to follow, and to relate parts of the evidence and testimony to the whole. It is not an occasion for argument." <u>United States v. Dinitz, 424</u> U.S. 600,612, 47 L.Ed. 2d 267,96 S. Ct. 1075(1976).

The next stage of the trial is the opening statement, which is very much the **Crossing of the Rubicon** [40] for the State because prosecutors must substantiate all evidence referenced during opening statements. If the prosecution were to reference evidence that could not be corroborated, defendants are then at liberty to request a mistrial pursuant to <u>United States v. Brockington,</u> 849 F.2d 872, 875 (4th Cir 1988). For this reason, it is imperative that during the opening statement, you be on alert for anything the prosecution says. <u>(United State v. Dinitz)</u>

It is widely believed that jurors unconsciously make up their minds about guilt or innocence after the initial opening statements, and while this may not be an absolute, it does entail how important first impressions are in trials. This makes opening statements very important to the defendant's defense. Ironically, defendants have no absolute right to opening statements at all, as the federal Constitution does not protect the right to have opening statements during trials. However, prosecutors understand how impactful an opening statement can be in the grand scheme of presenting their theory to the jury, so rarely will there be an instance where prosecutors forgo this opportunity, also entitling defendants to the same opportunity. Prosecutors will always opt to provide an opening statement, as they know this is the most pivotal chance to paint a picture of their theory of facts in a way jurors will most readily identify with. The best way to describe this situation is by looking at it like a jigsaw puzzle. During the opening the statement, the prosecutors will impose on the jury what the picture of the puzzle will eventually look like when all of the pieces come together. Prosecutors will use the opening statement to describe all of the pieces they have collected, how all of the pieces fit together and attempt to justify why the picture may possibly come out flawed or incomplete in the end. This aspect of the trial serves to benefit prosecutors much more than it could defendants by virtue of the prosecution having the proverbial burden of proof. If prosecutors had no opening statement, they would have to rely solely on witness testimony and physical evidence to frame their theory of facts. This would then make it very difficult, as both physical evidence and witness testimony are susceptible to becoming invalid and unreliable through the Rules of Evidence. Without opening statements, prosecutors cannot adequately frame their theory, leaving the jury the responsibility of putting the pieces of the puzzle together for themselves. In hindsight, the absence of an opening statement would probably make this process fairer for many defendants where there is a lot of evidence but not much of a circumstantial case.

More than anything else, this further necessitates that you approach the opening statement with the same mentality as the prosecutor. You and your attorney must use this opening statement as a medium to paint the picture of your jigsaw puzzle; describing to the jury each piece of the puzzle and how they all fit perfectly to substantiate your picture, your theory, and your defense. So essentially what this means is whoever frames their theory the clearest during the opening statement will most likely have gained the advantage going into the war.

4). *Presentation of the Evidence*

The next stage of the trial is the presentation of the evidence. During this phase, both you and the prosecutor have an opportunity to present both physical and testimonial evidence. Each party will have the opportunity to rebut the evidence/testimony presented by the other side. If you put a witness on the stand, after you examine that witness, the State would then be able to cross-examine that witness in rebuttal. Afterwards, you could again offer a rebuttal to their rebuttal and vice versa. The State also has this same right with any witness you put on the stand.

This part of the trial is usually the most critical for

defendants as prosecutors will put witnesses on the stand for nothing more but to enflame the passions of the jury. In trials, two types of witnesses are almost impossible to overcome, the testimony of a child and the sobbing witness. The material weight of these two types of witnesses seem minimal but their emotional impact on a jury is always immeasurable. The emotional impact of the child and sobbing witness oftentimes clouds the jury's ability to reason by triggering their emotions. Anytime juries begin operating on pure emotion, it becomes less likely they will objectively identify with any theory of the defendant. The only way to overcome these hurtles is by attempting to challenge the admissibility of such testimony before such witnesses are put on the stand. When the State is examining a witness, you know will likely be emotional, you must not allow prosecutors to frame questions in a way to incite or inadvertently illicit emotional reactions from the witness. Prosecutors will also question instigate so that witnesses must explain traumatic experiences in graphic detail, knowing it will likely bring about emotional outbursts. When this happens, you should make it a point to object on the grounds of the prosecution trying to enflame the passions of the jury.

Anytime prosecutors examine witnesses on the stand, you should always know what elements of the charge the prosecutor's line of questioning is aiming to satisfy and secondly how such testimony stands to contradict the circumstantial theory of your defense. The intent behind all of the prosecutor's questions will always be relative to the elements of the charge. During the examination of witnesses, defendants should remain aware of how testimony is weighing on the elements, so one can immediately rebuff and rebut it. Understanding how to navigate testimonial evidence during the trial is a psychological cat and mouse game you must always be in tune with. All testimonial evidence is purposeful as witnesses cannot just get on the stand and offer testimony aimlessly. Testimony can only come about through probing and stimulating the right questions. For this reason, a certain cadence is necessary during witness examinations. If prosecutors can establish this rhythm, the witness's testimony will most likely substantiate some if not all of the elements at hand. Therefore, your goal as the defendant is to disrupt the prosecution's rhythm through the act of objection. The Black's Law dictionary defines objection as, "A formal statement opposing something that has occurred, or is about to occur, in court and seeking the judge's immediate ruling on the point." This is the first component of the objection; the second is to preserve the record for appeal, (which will be discussed later.) By asserting an objection during the examination of a witness, this will sometimes interrupt the prosecutor's line of questioning and train of thought. Defendants are never to do this in a belligerent fashion; **the purpose of this is not to make a mockery of the court.** The purpose of this tactic is to distract prosecutors from corroborating key points that make up an element. If you can render a prosecutor remiss in extracting key pieces of testimony from a witness, you thereby render that evidence obsolete. The intent behind objecting to something during a trial is to remove it from the consideration of the jury. So anytime either the defendant or the prosecutor makes an objection, there must be a valid reason provided. If valid, the judge will sustain it and correct the matter. Otherwise, it will be overruled, and the trial will continue as if the objection never occurred. While your true intent is interference when objecting, you should always have a valid reason in doing so in which to engage the prosecutor in some type of an exchange. This exchange could potentially serve as the intervening cause capable of shifting the focus of the prosecutors questioning altogether. Because to object and have the judge sustain your objections could also accomplish this tactic. I call this legal ideate element divergence [41] and again, <u>it is only possible if all of one's objections are relatively valid,</u> thus causing element divergence to occur inadvertently. This tactic may seem unethical, but no less ethical than the prosecutor's tactic of Jury Socialization. There are also many more tactics accessible to defendants if one remembers to do so under the guidance of the elements of the charge and the rules of engagement. After each party has examined their witnesses, and introduced their evidence this marks the 'close of the evidence', which denotes that at this point, no more evidence can be presented to the jury.

5). *Directed Verdict*

At this point, defendants could raise any Motions for Mistrial, Motions to Dismiss or Motions for Directed Verdict. The Black's Law Dictionary defines Directed Verdict as, "A ruling by a trial judge taking a case from the jury because the evidence will permit only one reasonable verdict." The court will only issue a directed verdict, 'when the evidence against a defendant is so lacking that no juror would reasonably convict of such." Or "if a verdict would be so palpable or flagrant against the evidence, so as to indicate that it was reached as a result of passion or prejudice." If the Court determines the evidence for a specific charge is not sufficient, the Court may grant a directed verdict motion thus acquitting you of that charge. As rare as it is to have these motions granted, your attorney should always file them as a matter of due diligence regardless of the likelihood of it being granted. And it would also be during this stage of the proceedings that you would submit your motion for a new trial based on any I.A.C. claims you may have, which will be explained further in the next chapter.

6). *Jury Instructions*

After the judge rules on all of these motions, next comes the drafting of the jury instructions, which unbeknownst to many is probably one of the most significant stages of the trial. It is imperative for all defendants to understand the fashion in which these instructions are constructed determines how juries' approach what they perceive to be the facts of the case, how they identify with those facts, and how they ultimately apply the elements to the facts. As mentioned earlier, prosecutors have an adversarial advantage by means of having their theory of facts always take precedence in the instructions. Oftentimes, the party most successful at influencing the theory of facts will win this war. If possible, you must at least attempt to draft the jury instructions in a way that is most conducive to your defense. You do not have to be a legal genius to create jury instructions, just make sure that the instructions you present include all of the elements of the charges. This is not to say the Court will always accept them, but the goal is to negotiate in a way that provides you with some control over how your jury instructions are constructed. This is something you should not just leave to your attorney. The right to participate in the drafting of your own jury instructions is a right you have under the Sixth Amendment of the United States Constitution. After all of the jury instructions are complete, next is the closing arguments.

7.) *Closing Argument*

Unlike the opening statement, the closing argument is a right guaranteed by the United States Constitution. Herring v. New York, 422 U.S. 853, 858, 955. Ct. 2550, 2553, 45 L. Ed. 2d 593 (1975) states:

> *"It can hardly be questioned, "that closing argument serves to sharpen and clarify the issues for resolution by the trier of fact in a criminal case. For it is only after all the evidence is in that counsel for the parties are able to present their respective versions of the case as a whole. Only then can they argue the inferences to be drawn from all the testimony and point out the weaknesses of their adversaries' positions. And for the defense, closing argument is the last clear*

chance to persuade the trier of fact that there may be reasonable doubt of the defendant's guilt."

In trials, the closing argument is the prosecution's last opportunity to bring all of

the pieces of the puzzle together into one final picture for the jury. Consequently, the prosecution's closing argument will always be emotional, awe inspiring, and Grammy worthy performances detailing how they have put together a perfect puzzle of the facts. Which will always be misleading. As important as closing arguments are for prosecutors, they are also just as important for defendants. It's routine for prosecutors to manipulate the closing statement as a means of enflaming the passions of the jury but also to transform complicated legislative elements into that of conceivable circumstantial elements. This makes it imperative for you and your attorney to convey to the jury in the closing argument the necessity of not just any circumstantial theory but a complete circumstantial theory. You and your attorney must convey to the jury that this theory must account for both logic as well as the elements of the charge. You must continuously reiterate how a logical theory is necessary if one is to reach **reasonable certainty** [42] in a verdict. <u>Because logic conveys that one cannot believe beyond a reasonable doubt unless one has believed with reasonable certainty.</u> By articulating to the jury the importance of reasonable certainty, it ensures that they don't just accept anything. Reasonable certainty serves as another way of understanding how reasonable doubt is to apply to the facts. And if successful, you may very well use the prosecutor's circumstantial theory against them. The objective is to establish to the jury that if there is no reasonable certainty as to the prosecution's theory, this eliminates reasonable doubt, which is a requisite to the finding of guilt of any defendant. For example, consider a case involving a defendant accused of shooting a man in a restaurant in which only the victim and the alleged shooter were present in at the time of the crime. Immediately after the shooting, police promptly arrest the alleged shooter and retrieve possible camera footage. However, because of the position of the camera, the footage does not show the actual shooting but does show that no one left or entered the restaurant after the shooting took place. In such a situation, reasonable certainty in the defendant's guilt should entail hearing testimony from the victim, but also the introduction of a murder weapon somewhere in the restaurant or on the suspect. This would be consistent with logic, as the murder weapon could not have just magically disappeared. Regardless of the elements of murder being present, a complete theory, which could account for all of the underlying facts, rather than just the elements, may be necessary to reach a state of reasonable certainty. If a jury were unable, through the evidence, to ascertain a complete narrative of all of the facts surrounding the crime, how much weight can the elements have? In the above example, by apprehending the suspect, in the restaurant, immediately after the shooting, logic and reasonable certainty would necessitate an explanation of why there was no murder weapon found. How can one logically determine guilt beyond a reasonable doubt when no circumstantial explanation exists for the absence of a murder weapon? However, as it stands, such an explanation is not required because of the way in which jury instructions have made the reasonable doubt standard obsolete.

During trials, most jurors by default do not consider a complete circumstantial theory because of how this process is structured. If this 'mysterious restaurant murder' were to happen in our criminal justice system, prosecutors would only justify this 'missing piece' by conveying to the jury that they do not have to explain or account for the absence of a murder weapon. They would explain how the law only requires they prove the elements of Murder and technically, they would be right. However, there is a grey area in this situation in which jurors could factor 'reasonable doubt' into the equation thus requiring an explanation of the murder weapon before they can reach a state of 'reasonable certainty'. But as I mentioned previously, the jury instructions that are typically drafted in this system omit reasonable doubt as an element of guilt and fails to explain it thus limiting how jurors can consider the facts. Therefore, one should artfully emphasize to the jury the importance of reasonable certainty, as well as the importance of a complete circumstantial theory. You must not allow the prosecutor to convince the jury that their theory is complete if that is not the case. You must demonstrate in the closing argument how the prosecution's theory is not complete. Because if juries deem the prosecution's theory complete, they will see no reason to consider any other theory. When this happens, the war is over, and you lose. In my opinion, the closing argument for defendants is a means of reiterating to the jury how the prosecution's theory of facts is not the burden of guilt. You must also at the same time use the closing argument to establish your circumstantial theory. After both the defendant and the prosecution make their closing arguments, next is the deliberation process, followed by the reading of the verdict.

8). *Verdict*

Next is the reading of the verdict. After the jury deliberates and a verdict is in, everyone in the courtroom except the judge will stand and the jury foreperson will read the verdict on the record.

9). *Sentencing Phase*

If the jury returns a guilty verdict, next is the Sentencing phase or the mitigation phase. In this phase, you will be given an opportunity to present to the judge any form of mitigating evidence that may prompt the judge to grant you some form of leniency as to how your sentence should be served. Because of the hubris nature of many judges, defendants who lose this battle is expected to present themselves in pathetic fashion, crying and clobbering at the court's feet for mercy, anything less and judges will deem you deserving of what you receive from the jury. Sometimes begging for mercy will not even make a difference and will serve merely to feed the ego of the court, which afterwards leads to a legal explanation of why they will not and should not grant you any type of compassion. After this mitigation phase, the judge will then schedule your final sentencing hearing. At this final sentencing hearing, you will receive your final judgement, which outlines how your sentence is to be served as mentioned in earlier chapters, this final judgment is the legal instrument that legally transfers your personhood into the custody of the Department of Corrections for the commencement of your sentence.

16

"THE END GAME"

The Appellate Process

For some odd reason, most defendants stake hope in the idea that appellate courts are some type of judicial saviors that balances the scales of justice by righting all of the wrongs that occur throughout this process. The idea of appellate judges being any less partial or biased than trial judges can be misleading. If anything, the judges on the appellate level will have more experience in constitutional law and more experience translates to judges being more adept at legitimizing constitutional violations that occur in a case. This means appellate courts are constantly aiming to plug up loopholes rather than create them. You must never rest your hopes on the discretion of these judges, as if their aim is to uphold what is morally right. No, the sole objective and priority of appellate judges is to uphold and sustain the integrity of their respective State Constitution, regardless of what is morally right or wrong. This makes most appellate judges no different from lifeless robots programmed by a system to carry out automatic functions. When appellate judges adjudicate appeals, they are not considering the issues they hear on appeal through the lens of compassion, mercy, and justice but through the lens of their personal interpretation of how the constitution upholds the argument of the State, regardless of what it means to your personal livelihood. Therefore, whether you win your appeal is often contingent on how a decision may come to affect other defendants in the future. This means sometimes, even when the State violates a defendant's constitutional rights; many defendants will still lose their appeal for no other reason than if relief were provided, it would then open the floodgates to having to provide many more defendants relief. These are the type of concerns appellate courts weigh when granting relief on appeals, even if justice takes a backseat. The reason being is the central theme and agenda for the appellate court is one word, precedent. Every decision made in the appellate court is to establish and protect existing precedent and further maintain the status quo and as a result, there have been many defendants denied relief, not on the merits of their argument, but because of a potential loophole, it would create for others.

Now, this may sound pessimistically bleak as if I am implying that it is impossible to win on appeal, but this is not the case. My intention is only to put things in the proper perspective, so you don't invest too much hope and expectation in the appeal process. Because the more hope defendants have in the appeal process, the less focus they will give to defending against the State throughout the trial. My hope is by revealing the true nature of the appeal process; it leads to you being more proactive to the extent of not having to rely on it at all.

What I'm saying is the chances of having your conviction reversed on appeal is not impossible but rather slim. However, you increase your chances by understanding the layout of the appeal process going into this fight, not after the fight is over.

The first thing to understand about this process is when appealing your case; you are essentially attacking your conviction and final judgment. If you were to win your appeal, it doesn't necessarily mean the entire case will be dismissed or done away with. Having your sentence reversed, vacated, or remanded entails the appellate court vacating the judgment that rendered you property of the State, and sending your case back to the trial court with instructions to remedy the constitutional violation in question before any further prosecution can take place. In most cases, winning your appeal merely re-sets the whole process over to the beginning. While many are quick to consider this a win, you must always remember such a decision has its risks. If it happens that you win your appeal, and the process starts over, there is a possibility the State could have an invested interest in securing your personhood. Which means, the State can take you to trial a second time, and upon conviction, give you a longer sentence than you received in the first trial. The 1949, United States Supreme Court held in Williams v. New York, 337 U.S. 241, 245 that:

> *We hold, therefore, that neither the double jeopardy provision nor the Equal Protection Clause imposes an absolute bar to a more severe sentence upon reconviction. A trial judge is not constitutionally precluded, in other words, from imposing a new sentence, whether greater or less than the original sentence in light upon the defendants' life, health, habits, conduct, and mental and moral propensities."*

This implies that any additional information or evidence that surfaces at the second trial such as *"a new presentence investigation, your prison record, other sources" Id. Pierce, 395 US. 711,* can all be used as a justification to impose a harsher sentence than your first one.

It is in Pierce v. North Carolina, *395 US. 711,* that the United States Supreme Court establishes that though a trial court can always impose a more severe sentence, it cannot be by vindictiveness. Or, in other words the trial court cannot retaliate against you with a harsher sentence simply because you won your appeal. To make sure defendants are not retaliated against for appealing their sentences, Pierce, supra, established that a trial court's reasons for imposing harsher sentences in a second trial must be *"based on upon objective information concerning identifiable conduct on the part of the defendant occurring after the time of the original sentencing proceeding."* Furthermore, Pierce v. North Carolina also establishes, *"the factual data upon which the increase is based must be made part of the record, so that the constitutional legitimacy of the increased sentence may be fully reviewed."* In a sense, the United States Supreme Court is establishing that trial courts should not be vindictive in giving harsher sentences when defendants win on appeal but simultaneously provides trial courts a specific vehicle to do just that if they justify it. Therefore, when appealing your case, be cautious of all of these variables that could come into play if you were to win.

But in most cases, when defendant's win an appeal, most defendants would have at that point served so much time that many prosecutors typically decide that another trial is not even worth it and opt to offer you a favorable plea bargain just to dispose of the case. The main point is the appeal process in the criminal justice system is not the end all, be all, many presume it to be. In some situations, it might not be your best option.

In all but a few states [43], the appeal process is generally the same. The specific order of appealing one's case after conviction goes as follows:

❖ A). The Direct Appeal & Discretionary Review of Direct appeal

❖ B). The United States Supreme Court Certiorari. (If necessary)

❖ C). The State Collateral Appeal & (Appellate Court Review of Collateral Appeal)

❖ D). The Federal Habeas Corpus & (Review of Federal District Court & Review of Federal Circuit Court of Appeals)

The Sixth Amendment of the United States Constitution guarantees every defendant found guilty at trial, a right to appeal that conviction. Additionally, defendants also have a right to representation on appeal. In my humble opinion, out of all of the post-conviction appeals, the first appeal, also called the direct appeal, offers the defendant the best chance at relief due to the fact it is a panel of justices deciding the appeal. Another reason is that this is the only appeal providing you with a constitutional right to an attorney. This is significant because appellate judges will naturally be more receptive to attorneys rather than pro se defendants. The higher the Court, the more dismissive, cynical, and hostile the judges tend to be towards pro se litigants. Again, I believe the mere idea of having those whom society deems to be criminals practicing law with the same capacity the average attorney does could easily come off despicable to some judges. How dare we "criminals" appropriate the very profession upon which their entire livelihood rests upon? How dare we ignorant criminals so readily comprehend the jargon that makes up this intricate justice system! To the judges in the criminal justice system this is an anomaly. For a distinguished judge to have to acknowledge the legal aptitude of a mere criminal could only thus relegate the prestige they attach to their illustrious legal expertise.

Therefore, the first and most important appeal for the defendant after trial is the direct appeal. This is "the appeal" defendants must pull out all of the stops for. Defendants are required to do very little during this appeal, as your trial lawyer is responsible for filing your notice of appeal after the conviction. Afterwards, the court automatically appoints you an attorney from the public defender's office. Some appellate attorneys will visit you at least once for nothing more but morale support. But typically, most appellate lawyers will merely inform you by letter that they've been assigned to represent you on appeal and that's it. Many appellate lawyers feel there is no reason to interact with defendants because after they have received your record, they have everything they need to file your direct appeal without having to interact with you. If there is some claim you would like to make sure your lawyer adds to your appeal or something you would like to make your attorney aware of, it is best to write a letter, but make a copy of the letter and send it both to your appeal lawyer and the appellate court clerk to add to the record. This way if you ever need to prove your lawyer went against your wishes, your letter is on the record. It is imperative defendants get the most out of their direct appeal because in my opinion all of the subsequent appeals that follow thereafter, begin to receive less and less consideration, which in turn decreases one's chances of relief. After the trial, time is of the essence for defendants. Knowing this, the criminal justice system has purposely constructed the appeal process to be a long and drawn-out process. The time it takes to wait on your appellate attorney to A). Draft and submit the appeal, b). Wait for the State Attorney to respond and c). Finally receive back an answer from the appellate court can be an average of about one and a half to 2-year process for each appeal.

After the appellate court decides on your direct appeal and it becomes final you must keep in mind, you are now on the clock, so you must work diligently to prepare your next appeal, but this time without an attorney's assistance. Which proves challenging because the next and most difficult appeal this system offers you is the Certiorari to the United States Supreme Court. For criminal defendants, this is by far the least reliable appeal of the four. What makes Certiorari appeals so unreliable is the United States Supreme Court handpicks which cases it will decide! Even if you manage to overcome all of the filing technicalities that come along with filing a Certiorari, there is still no guarantee the United States Supreme Court will accept your Certiorari to review. The following will give you an idea of the nature of this appeal.

> *"It is important to note that review in this Court by means of a writ of certiorari is not a matter of right, but of judicial discretion. The primary concern of the Supreme Court is not to correct errors in lower court decisions, but to decide cases presenting issues of importance beyond the particular facts and parties involved. The Court grants and hears argument in only about 1% of the cases that are filed each Term. The vast majority of petitions are simply denied by the Court without comment or explanation. The denial of a petition for a writ of certiorari signifies only that the Court has chosen not to accept the case for review and does not express the Court's view of the merits of the*

case."

—OFFICE OF THE CLERK, SUPREME COURT OF THE UNITED STATES

This means this court is particularly not looking to save you from whatever injustice there is in your case, but rather to only reconcile any conflicts existing in the lower and Federal courts. When filing this Certiorari, one can only hope for relief if it serves the Courts purpose. Nonetheless, if you happen to have a violation of your federal rights and it's an issue that you researched and found to be inconclusive in the lower courts throughout various Federal circuits, this appeal may be something you should consider. You have exactly 90 days from the day your direct appeal becomes final to file a Certiorari to the United States Supreme Court, as filing it would also toll other appeal deadlines from all other courts. However, you must carefully think about your claims, and decide whether they are even worth taking to the United States Supreme Court. As mentioned earlier, you should consider caselaw and determine whether your claims fall in the category of what the United States Supreme Court seeks. And if so, this appeal might be ideal for you. But, if your claims rest purely on State law, or if there is already leading caselaw that resolves the issues that make up your claims, you might also need to think about whether skipping this appeal is your best option because it just may be. Make no mistake, I'M NOT TELLING YOU TO SKIP THIS APPEAL. I am merely telling you that there are certain claims one should not waste the time of trying to bring to this court. The ultimate decision is up to you.

Nonetheless, if you were to appeal and not prevail on Certiorari or decide to skip it, next, is the State collateral appeal. The purpose of the State Collateral Appeal is to provide the defendant with a means to argue any claim you could not argue on direct appeal. It is through the State collateral appeal that defendants argue the infamous I.A.C. claims which is "Ineffective Assistance of Counsel [44]". However, in many States, defendants can present their I.A.C. claims on their direct appeal. You should familiarize yourself with the direct appeal rules of your State as well as caselaw to find out if you can argue I.A.C. claims on your direct appeal. I.A.C [45]. are claims of poor performance of your attorney throughout your case. If the courts deems that your attorney's performance was constitutionally deficient, your respective State and Federal Constitution mandates you to be given a new trial. Most defendants will have been represented by State appointed attorneys, who because of their heavy workload, are unable to render every client their full commitment, which makes ineffective assistance of counsel probably the most common claim made on appeal. In most States, these State collateral appeals will first be heard in the trial court you were sentenced and if denied further appealed to the State Appellate Court. See the Rules of Appellate procedure in your State for details.

After the State collateral appeal is fully exhausted, the next appeal is the Petition for Writ of Federal Habeas Corpus. One must also be very careful with these appeals because there are a number of technicalities that stand to preclude the federal court from considering your petition. One of the more common technicalities of the Federal Habeas Corpus many defendants stumble with is the one-year rule. All Federal Habeas Petitions are subject to Federal Rule 28 U.S.C. 2244(d), which entails that defendants have exactly _one-year_ after their direct appeal becomes final to file the Federal Habeas Corpus. [46] However, this one-year deadline is always paused and is not in effect while you have your state collateral appeal pending. This means, as soon the Supreme Court issues the final order of your direct appeal, you should promptly begin preparing and filing your state collateral appeal to stop this one-year clock. Every second you take preparing your state collateral appeal counts against this one-year Federal habeas Corpus. This means, after your direct appeal, if it takes you 10 months to file your state collateral appeal, you would then have only 2 months remaining to file your federal habeas corpus before this one-year elapses and the federal court refuses to consider your habeas corpus. Another common default defendants run into is attempting to argue rights and claims that are solely protected by State Constitutions rather than the Federal Constitution. The United States

Supreme Court establishes in caselaw pursuant to Estelle v. McGuire, 505 U.S. 62, that, *"([I]n federal court, there is no right to bring a habeas Petition on the basis of a violation of State law.") Federal habeas relief is not available for attacks on violations of slate law or procedure and is unavailable for alleged error in the interpretation or application of State law.* In the past, I have personally stumbled with this default. A lot of times we get so caught up in litigating our arguments we don't even stop to consider whether the Federal Constitution even provides relief for what I'm arguing. Because if not, there is no use in arguing it in a Federal Habeas Corpus because courts will not provide relief if it doesn't.

Another technicality Federal courts commonly deny habeas corpus appeals for is failing to fill out the 2254 **Habeas Corpus form.** [47] Unlike other appeals, when you file a federal Habeas Corpus defendants are required to complete a form, which looks a lot like an application. You must answer every question in this form in entirety. Any question you fail to answer can be a means of the Federal court refusing to hear that claim on appeal.

Anytime you file a 2254 Writ for Habeas Corpus, you must include this application along with your actual motion.

Infact, defendants are not even required to submit an actual motion along with the Petition because the Petition itself is the actual Writ, but it is always better to do so anyway. Drafting a motion along with the application provides you a more in depth means to litigate your arguments.[48] When you file your Habeas Corpus, a district judge will hear it, and if denied; Federal caselaw establishes,

> *"A State prisoner whose petition/or a writ of habeas corpus is denied by a Federal District Court does not enjoy an absolute right to appeal. Federal law requires that the first obtain a certificate of appealability (COA) from a circuit justice or judge. 28 U.S.C.S 2253 (c){l). A COA may issue only if the applicant has made a substantial showing of the denial of a constitutional right. 28 U.S.C.S 2253*

(c)(2). Until the prisoner secures a COA, the Court of Appeals may not rule on the merits of his case. Miller-El v. Cockrell, 537 U.S. 322 (2003).

This means, if the District Court denies you a Certificate of Appealability, you can thereafter try to appeal that denial to the Federal Circuit Court of Appeals, but that Court does not have to consider the merits of your claims without a C.O.A from the lower courts. If the Federal Circuit Court does, consider your claims and still does not provide you with relief that would be the end of your Federal Habeas Corpus appeals. After the federal habeas corpus, there are no other Courts in which to seek relief from your conviction. If something happens relative to new evidence in your case, there are certain avenues every State provides for such situations. In most instances, this process is designed in such a way that when a defendant finally reaches this stage, you will most likely have served more than half of the time it takes to typically be eligible for some type of release.

EXCLUSIVE
"SET THE RECORD STRAIGHT!"

If you happen to be in certain States and you are looking to do something to speed this appeal process up, there may be a possible way to cut some time off this process by a legal ideate I call *Setting the Record Straight* [49]. The basis of this idea is from <u>United States v. Rodriguez,</u> 675 F. 3d 48, 57-58(1st Cir.2012) where the appellate court acknowledges that:

> "There is a narrow exception to this rule when the defendant raises an objection at trial or when the trial record clearly reflects grounds for the ineffective assistance of counsel claim."

As mentioned earlier, the first two appeals afforded to defendants are the direct appeal and the Certiorari. This idea of Setting the Record Straight entails you first preparing your trial record in such a way that enables you to argue your I.A.C. claims in your direct appeal rather than having to wait and argue them on State Collateral appeals. Now, the advantages of incorporating I.A.C. claims into your direct appeal are:

A). You would have the luxury of having an attorney argue not just your typical direct appeal claims, but also your I.A.C. claims as well.

B). You would have an opportunity to present your I.A.C claims in a higher state court rather than having to first argue them in a lower court.

C). And if unsuccessful, you would still have an opportunity to argue any *I.A.A.C.* [50] claims on State Collateral appeal, if necessary.

Now there are some states that allow and encourage you to file I.A.C. claims on the direct appeal. But in the States that discourage it, the first court that will hear your claims of I.A.C. will normally be the trial court. If the trial court denies these claims, you can afterwards appeal those claims to a State appellate court. However, by adding your I.A.C. claims to your direct appeal, you then have the advantage of skipping the trial court and taking your I.A.C claims directly to the highest State appellate court for determination. By doing such, you save time because unlike Direct Appeals, State collateral appeals can drag out much longer in appeal courts. The reason being is State collateral appeals have less protection regarding time due to the Federal Constitution not guaranteeing defendants a right to a prompt State collateral appeal. The Federal Courts in Montgomery v. Meloy, 90 F. 3d 1200 holds that:

> Mere delay in receiving a ruling on a state petition for post- conviction relief does not violate the Due Process Clause. Although the inexcusable delay in processing a direct criminal appeal may violate due process, the same does not hold true for delay in processing a collateral appeal. Due Process does not include prompt resolution of collateral appeals.

Those who decide to take the normal route will have to wait to have their I.A.C claims heard and denied in the trial court, only to then appeal to the State appellate court, which resets this 2-3-year process all over again. But, by Setting the Record Straight, and adding these claims to your direct appeal, you save yourself at least 2-3 years' time. Of Course, the system is aware of how this tactic could greatly benefit the defendant and as a result, all of the appellate Judges on every level discourage defendants from presenting these claims on direct appeal. The appellate courts have always used the same unconvincing reasons to discourage defendants from presenting I.A.C claims on direct appeal which the United States Supreme Court illustrates in <u>Massaro v. United States,</u> 538 U.S. 500 in its holding:

> "When a claim is brought on direct appeal, appellate counsel and the court must proceed on a trial record that is not developed precisely for, and is therefore often incomplete or

inadequate for, the purpose of litigating or preserving the claim. A defendant claiming ineffective counsel must show that counsel's actions were not supported by a reasonable strategy and that the error was prejudicial. The evidence introduced at trial, however, will be devoted to guilt or innocence issues, and the resulting record may not disclose the facts necessary to decide either prong of the Strickland analysis..."

Nonetheless, this language is only a discouragement and not an impairment. The true reasoning behind all appellate courts discouraging defendants from arguing I.A.C. claims on direct appeal is because they claim the trial record is not developed. Which makes no sense at all. This is to imply that nothing in the trial record holds verification of whether these claims are material or immaterial. This logic expressed in Massaro, supra, comes of nonsensical, as if the trial record magically develops or changes after your direct appeal becomes final. In caselaw, the North Carolina Supreme Court attempts to offer a more in-depth premise as to the meaning of the trial record being inadequate, which is no less absurd to say the least.

> "Resolving an IAC claim frequently requires *information that necessarily is not a part of the record* at trial, namely whether trial counsel made a conscious choice to pursue a given strategy, why that strategy was chosen, and whether that choice was reasonable, Thus, "because of the nature IAC (Ineffective Assistance of Counsel) claims defendants likely will not be in a position to adequately develop many IAC claims on direct appeal." State v. Fair, 354 N.C. 131, 167 557 S. E. 2d

500, 525

The reasoning offered in the above case is ridiculous. Information such as an attorney's trial strategy and its reasonableness are not developed in the direct appeal process. In fact, aside from the Supreme Court's opinion, the record will be no different than it was after the trial. The truth of the matter is after the conclusion of the trial; the record is as developed as it ever will be. Regarding the *"information that is not part of the record"* mentioned in State v. Fair, such information can only be ascertained through I.A.C. evidentiary hearings. If the North Carolina Supreme Court speaks for the majority, what this implies is every single defendant who argues ineffective assistance of counsel on appeal is entitled to an I.A.C evidentiary hearing to determine an attorney's trial strategy, otherwise a reasonable determination of these claims are impossible. If this is true, thousands upon thousands of defendants are thus entitled to retroactive evidentiary hearings because every day appellate courts on the State and federal level are denying appeals arguing I.A.C. claims without ever ascertaining "from the record" such questions. No, this "inadequacy of the record" excuse has nothing to do with why appellate courts discourage defendants from presenting these claims on direct appeal. This nonsensical excuse cannot be valid, as Courts have regularly contradicted this. For example, in State collateral proceedings in Missouri, Florida, Arkansas and Kentucky, it is generally held that a defendant is not entitled to relief for I.A.C. claims if:

> "the record conclusively showed that his ineffective assistance of counsel claims were not plausible."

Countless defendants lose their appeal and any chance of an evidentiary hearing for this very reason. Now, how could on one hand the trial record be inadequate and too premature for courts to ascertain I.A.C. claims on direct appeal, but on the other hand, just as soon as the direct appeal becomes final this same record then becomes sufficient to determine that such claims are not even worthy of an evidentiary hearing? How blatantly inconsistent is this? No, the real reason such claims are discouraged from being presented on direct appeal is possibly because 1). It would create more work for already understaffed and overworked public defenders, which would further deplete judicial resources, 2). It would create an ethical dilemma of forcing attorneys to challenge the integrity and merit of other attorneys, and 3). It would create more work for Court justices on direct appeals. Nevertheless, it is not our responsibility to help the system. This is a war, and all is fair in war.

HOW TO SET THE RECORD STRAIGHT?

Therefore, the *only* way to "Set the Record Straight" as mentioned earlier, is to provide the appellate court a basis on the record through which to consider these claims. This further provides them with no excuse not to hear these claims on direct appeal. Preparing the trial record for I.A.C claims consists of two things: 1). Objecting and expressing on the record anything your attorney does that harms your defense or your rights and 2). At the close of evidence, filing a motion for a new trial with arguments and caselaw that outlines how your attorney's performance was ineffective and also requesting an evidentiary hearing. The main goal behind trying to obtain an evidentiary hearing is to expand the record for your I.A.C. claims if a direct appeal becomes necessary.

When arguing I.A.C. claims, you must first understand the standard caselaw provides to prove ineffective assistance of counsel. Any and every constitutional violation will always have a set standard that must be substantiated to prevail on such claims. The standard which caselaw provides for I.A.C. violations is the Strickland standard, which derives from Strickland v. Washington, 466 U.S. 668, 104 S. Ct. 2052, 80 L.Ed.2d 674. The Strickland standard is a two- prong test that entails you demonstrating:

1. That counsel's representation was deficient in that it fell below an objective standard of reasonableness, measured against prevailing professional norms,

2. That the defendant was prejudiced by his attorney's deficient performance. Strickland v. Washington, 466 U.S. 668 (1984)

In simple terms, this means you must demonstrate 1). Your attorney did something during or before the trial that was so irrational to common sense that it is contrary to what any other normal attorney would have done under similar circumstances. And 2). The error was so egregious it violated your constitutional right to a fair trial. The only way to understand how difficult this standard can be to prove is by reading all of the caselaws in which the appellate courts have denied I.A.C. claims for failing to meet this standard. It is only after studying the necessary caselaw that you understand what you must establish to prevail on these claims. In a trial, your focus must be on both getting acquitted and preparing for a potential appeal. This is what it means to hope for the best but prepare for the worst. Preparing for the worst includes, evaluating, and considering all of the things you can use to satisfy the Strickland standard during the trial. This also includes saving anything your attorney sends you and collecting their entire work product during the case as well as after. Many *I.A.C.* claims come down to nothing more than proving them, which in some cases is more difficult than meeting the actual Strickland standard. The success of having the trial court entertain your I.A.C. claims is contingent on how much merit you provide your arguments. To give you an idea of the "logic" that applies in I.A.C claims, the following cases will assist you.

1. United States v. Gray, 878 F. 2d 702,711 (3d Cir. 1989)

2. Missouri v. Frye, 566 U.S. 134

3. Hilton v. Alabama, 571 U.S. 263

4. Woods v. Donald, 575 U.S. 312

5. Buck v. Davis, 580 U.S. 100

6. Rompilla v. Beard, 545 U.S. 374

7. Lafler v. Cooper, 566 U.S. 156

8. Wiggins v. Smith, 539 U.S. 156

9. <u>Lee v. United Stated</u>. 137 S. Ct. 1958.

You should also look for caselaw from your respective State regarding I.A.C. claims.

There is an example motion in the back of the book **(see attachment 2)** providing you a basis on how to construct a motion for new trial you would tile during the trial as you attempt to Set the Record Straight. The general language of the example motion should be useful in creating your own motion, but obviously, you would have to finesse it by substituting your own relative information rather than using the Kentucky Layout. By presenting this motion to the court at the close to all of the evidence, this preserves these claims on appeal. If the judge happens to grant you an evidentiary hearing or even rules on the motion at all during the trial, this could only help in Setting the Record in a way the appellate courts have no choice but acknowledge. If it so happens that the trial court refuses to acknowledge it, filing it still preserves these issues on the record. As mentioned earlier, the second way of Setting the Record Straight so appellate courts have a sufficient basis to review your

I.A.C claims on direct appeal is by objecting on the record throughout the pretrial and trial. But, because you have an attorney representing you, it is best to do this with finesse, so you do not come off as a distraction or nuisance to the Court. Hence, my advice is to write a letter to the judge before the trial begins, expressing that pursuant to <u>United States v.</u> <u>Medina-Anicacio,</u> 325 F.3d 638, you would like to establish a process of presenting in writing all objections you personally have throughout the trial regarding your attorney's performance. This motion must be filed at the 'close of the evidence' along with the motions you file for a directed verdict. (See **attachment 3, for example letter).**

One of the advantages about attempting to Set the Record Straight is even if you are not successful in having your I.A.C claims heard on direct appeal, you still could argue these claims, albeit in the normal fashion in State collateral appeals. You also have the luxury of watching how the trial plays out, studying caselaw, and determining if there are reasonable I.A.C. claims in your case before deciding to present them in your direct appeal. If there are substantial claims you can utilize, you can then present them in a motion for new trial after the closing of all of the evidence.

Now beware, if you prevail in Setting the Record Straight and can successfully present your I.A.C claims on direct appeal, this will further preclude you from arguing those same I.A.C claims on your state collateral appeal afterwards. Because once the higher court rules on these claims, the lower court is in no position to hear them afterwards, so this prevents you from being able to re-raise these same claims. However, as previously mentioned, you do have the opportunity on State Collateral appeals to argue any *I.A.A.C* (Ineffective Assistance of Appellate Counsel Claims) which are claims that your <u>appellate attorney</u> was ineffective in representing you on appeal. Ineffective Assistance of Appellate Counsel claims are much like Strickland. The only nuance with I.A.A.C claims is that you must prove the Strickland Standard as well as:

(1) appellate counsel's performance was deficient; and (2) the deficient

performance prejudiced the defense. See id. However, several Courts have held that in an Anders context. Where appellate counsel must submit a brief advising the Court of anything in the record that is arguably meritorious, a defendant need not satisfy the prejudice prong. See, e.g., <u>Evans v. Clarke</u>, 868 F. 2d 267, 268 (8ᵗʰ Cir. 1989).

Therefore, if your appellate lawyer somehow drops the ball in properly arguing any of your claims on direct appeal, you can appeal under Ineffective assistance of appellate counsel in the State court and if valid, the trial Court may grant you another attorney to help represent you on your State collateral appeal. Maybe.... But, beware, because some States do not recognize these I.A.A.C claims, which preclude you from arguing them on State Collateral appeals, so you should research caselaw to find out if your State recognizes I.A.A.C claims before attempting to present them in State Collateral appeals. If you, by chance fail to prevail on these claims also, you are then able to appeal all your I.A.C. claims, I.A.A.C claims, and all of the other constitutional claims made in your direct appeal to the Federal Court through a Petition for Writ of Federal Habeas Corpus. And even if you do not prevail in setting the record straight, what you can take pride in is, having helped pave the way for others to take this same path, much to the dismay of the criminal justice system as your path would become caselaw for all to acknowledge. After such, you would be gratified to know that you were able to blaze a trail someone else could follow in the future. I had to learn all of this through trial and error, with no guidance and ultimately understood much of it after it was too late. For that reason, I have taken my own advice, using my experience to help those corning behind me so others do not continue to suffer for our lack of knowledge of this system.

When applying this during trial, you should expect a lot of resistance from both the prosecutor and the judge as one goes about Setting the Record Straight. Do not allow this resistance to disrupt your composure, because such resistance may bring about additional issues you can use for the record or for additional claims on appeal. If you can successfully Set the Record Straight, the appeal process should then be as follows:

    A). **The Direct Appeal.** (With I.A.C. claims included)

    ❖ B). **The United States Supreme Court Certiorari.** (if necessary)

    C). **The State Collateral Appeal.** (Arguing only, I.A.A.C claims)

    D). **The Federal Habeas Corpus** (2254) (Arguing Direct Appeal Claims, I.A.C claims, and I.A.A.C claims)

In conclusion, it is important you approach the appellate process understanding it is a very technical process. Each appellate Court will have its own rules for filing an appeal. Tread cautiously when it comes to filing these appeals on your own. Always research and thoroughly familiarize yourself with the court rules that apply to the appeal you're filing. And most importantly, never, ever wait until the last minute to start preparing your appeal. While any appeal you have is pending, you should always start preparing the next appeal just in case that appeal is unsuccessful, that way you can promptly submit the next one having lost no time in the process. By filing your appeals punctually, you avoid having your appeals dismissed or procedurally defaulted [51] because you fail to comply with filing deadlines. This is like a soldier dying on the way to battle. This should never be the case. Get in the habit of fact checking what you hear regarding the law. Do not just rely on what this book or what anybody tells you for that matter. Research to confirm or deny everything you hear regarding the legal process in your situation. The familiarization of four components of this criminal justice system will ready you for this fight as nothing else ever can. These components are your respective State Court rules, State Penal Statutes, State Constitutional Amendments, and caselaw. **Now make no mistake,** this book is not a legal authority you can cite in court to support your argument. If you were to try citing any of the 'legal ideates' provided in this book, the courts would not acknowledge them. I have constructed many of these ideas to provide defendants with a means to see this system for what it is. Therefore, I have created this book to be a guide but most importantly, a lens through which to offer defendants a better perspective of this process. A perspective that I hope will provide you with a much-needed advantage in this long and arduous fight you have ahead of you. My hope is after reading this book; you become what I call Finessed. May whatever God you worship, protect you and bring you home to your family as soon as possible.

Peace and Blessings

- Swan

EXHIBITS GUIDE

"The criminal justice process is set up in a way that misleads people from the beginning. This begins with the "Defendant" label you are assigned. By assigning you this label, it falsely conveys the idea that the defendant's victory can only come about by approaching your case on the defense."

-Swan

ATTACHMENT ONE
EXAMPLE MOTION

COMMONWEALTH OF KENTUCKY

JEFFERSON COUNTY CIRCUIT COURT

CASE NO. 00-CR-000000

JOHN DOE   MOVANT

VS.

COMMONWEALTH OF KENTUCKY   RESPONDENT

MOTION TO SUPPRESS EVIDENCE OF UNLAWFUL SEARCH PURSUANT TO AND SECTION 12 OF THE KENTUCKY CONSTITUTION AND THE FOURTH AMENDMENT OF UNITED STATES CONSTITUTIONS

Comes now the Defendant, John Doe, *prose*, and in good faith, and hereby moves this Honorable Court to Suppress Evidence as a result illegal search and seizure in the above listed case number pursuant to Fourth Amendment of the United States Constitution and Section 12 of Kentucky Constitution. As grounds for this request, Defendant states as follows:

(1). Meece v. Commonwealth, 348 S.W. 3d 627, 659 (Ky.

2011) has held that: In its fourth Amendment Context, in order for a defendant to invoke "the fruit of the poisonous tree doctrine," a "defendant must show that "(1) he or she has standing to challenge the original violation, i.e., the tree; (2) the original police activity violated his or her rights; and (3) the evidence sought to be admitted against him or her, i.e., the fruit, was obtained as a result of the original violation." A Court will, however, admit the fruit of the poisonous tree if the prosecutor establishes that (1) the evidence was obtained from a source independent of the primary illegality; (2) the evidence inevitably would have been discovered in the course of the investigation; or (3) the connection the challenged evidence and the illegal conduct is so attenuated that it dissipates the taint of the illegal action." Id

(2) The defendant argues and can demonstrate as follows that in this situation, all of the above elements required to invoke this fruit of the poison tree doctrine are present and for this reason all evidence seized as a result of the unlawful search and seizure must be suppressed.

WHEREFORE, for the foregoing reasons, the Movant prays this honorable court issue and ORDER directing that a suppression hearing be held in this case.

Respectfully Submitted,

_____
Defendant, pro se

VERIFICATION

I hereby verify that all of the information contained in this motion is true and correct to the best of my knowledge and belief at this time.

_____

John Doe, Affiant

NOTICE

Please take notice that the foregoing motion has been filed in the:

Jefferson Clerk of Circuit & District Courts
David Nicholson
Hall of Justice
600 W Jefferson St. 2nd Fl
Louisville, KY 4020-2740

                                           on this _____ day of _____

                                           _____

                                           John Doe, pro se

CERTIFICATE OF SERVICE

This is to certify that a true and correct copy of the foregoing has been mailed to:

Jefferson Commonwealth Attorney
Thomas B. Wine
514 W Liberty St
Louisville, KY 40202-2800

on this _____ day of _____

_____

John Doe, pro se

(To ensure that your motions are properly filed into the record, one should always send a copy to both the Clerk of the Court, prosecuting attorney's office and deliver a copy directly to the judge by hand, through the court bailiff.)

ATTACHMENT TWO
"EXAMPLE MOTION"

COMMONWEALTH OF KENTUCKY
JEFFERSON COUNTY CIRCUIT COURT
CASE NO. 00-CR-0000

JOHN DOE   DEFENDANT

MOTION TO REVERSE, VACATE OR REMAND JUDGMENT ON THE GROUNDS OF INEFFECTIVE ASSISTANCE OF COUNSEL
VS.
PURSUANT TO SECTION ONE OF THE KENTUCKY CONSTITUTION AND SIXTH AND FOURTEENTH AMENDMENT OF THE UNITED STATES CONSTITUTIONS

COMMONWEALTH OF KENTUCKY   RESPONDENT

* * *   * * *   * * *

Comes now the Defendant, John Doe, pro se and in good faith moves this honorable Court pursuant to Strickland V. Washington and any and all other applicable provisions of the Kentucky and United States Constitutions to grant the Defendant a New Trial.

1). Counsel was ineffective and the Defendant was deprived of his rights under the 6th and 14th Amendments of the U.S. Constitution were counsel failed to:

(EXAMPLE CLAIMS)

A). Adequately investigate and prepare an adequate defense.

B. Failed to subpoena witness key witnesses.

C). Failed to Suppress Evidence.

    2) Defendant moves this Honorable Court to set this matter for an "Evidentiary Hearing" as a means to develop the record for direct appeal purposes.

    3) Defendant also moves this honorable Court to *appoint separate counsel* for the purpose of conducting a **review** of the record, and if deemed necessary, supplementing the pleadings, and representing the Movant during any hearings held.

    5) At the conclusion of these proceedings, the Defendant moves this honorable Court to make *"Findings of Fact and Conclusions of Law"* concerning all of the issues presented herein with regard to the State and Federal Constitutional claims involved.

    WHEREFORE, it is requested that this Honorable Court grant a New Trial based on claims raised in this motion, or in the alternate, to set this matter for an evidentiary hearing, after appointing the Department of Public Advocacy to conduct a **review** of this claim, in advance of possibly supplementing the pleadings, and representing the defendant during any hearings held.

    Respectfully Submitted,

_____

John Doe, Defendant, pro se

VERIFICATION

I hereby verify that all of the information contained in this motion is true and correct to the best of my knowledge and belief at this time.

_____

John Doe, Affiant

NOTICE

Please take notice that the foregoing motion has been filed in

Jefferson Clerk of Circuit & District Courts
David Nicholson
Hall of Justice
600 W Jefferson St. 2nd Fl
Louisville, KY 4020-2740

on this_ day of _____

_____
John Doe, pro se

CERTIFICATE OF SERVICE

This is to certify that a true and correct copy of the foregoing has been mailed to:

Jefferson Commonwealth Attorney
Thomas B. Wine
514 W Liberty St
Louisville, KY 40202-2800

on this ___ day of _____

_____
John Doe, <u>pro se</u>

(To ensure that your motions are properly filed into the record, one should always send a copy to both the Clerk of the Court, prosecuting attorney's office and deliver a copy directly to the judge by hand, through the court bailiff.)

ATTACHMENT THREE
(EXAMPLE LETTER)

Honorable Judge,

My name is John Doe, a defending party to a pending case in your courtroom, case number: _____. I am writing because I would like to inform the Court that throughout the case/trial, my attorney will be submitting objections for various reasons, but I also will be submitting my own objections as well. It is not my intention to intrude on my attorney's representation or interrupt the court proceedings in any way. I have opted to submit all my objections to the court 'in writing' pursuant to <u>United States v. Neal,</u> 578 F. 3d 270 and <u>United States v. Medina-Anicacio</u>, 325 F.3d 638, 642(5th Cir.) which I will deliver through the Court bailiff at the conclusion of each court proceeding. The purpose for this letter is not to dismiss my attorney's performance as of now. but to establish a preservation mechanism for any issues or errors that may arise through his/her performance throughout the case/trial in a way that does not make a mockery of the court. This letter stems from my intention to develop the record, not as a matter of inconvenience to this court I hope, but as a matter of my constitutional right pursuant to <u>Tussey</u>

v. ABB Inc., 2015 U.S. Dist. LEXIS 89068 and also Griffin V. United States. 330 F. 3d 733, 739 (6th Cir 2003.) I ask that this letter be submitted to the record and that all of my written objections, if necessary, be duly accepted and submitted to the record also. Thank you for your time and consideration in this matter.

Sincerely,

_____

John Doe

(To ensure that your letter is properly filed into the record, one should always send a copy to both the Clerk of the Court, prosecuting attorney's office and deliver a copy directly to the judge by hand, through the court bailiff.)

ATTACHMENT FOUR

(Example Writ)

PETITION UNDER 28 U.S.C § 2254 FOR WRIT OF
HABEAS CORPUS BY A PERSON IN STATE CUSTODY

United States District Court	District:
Name (under which you were convicted):	Docket or Case No:
Place of Confinement	Prisoner No:
Petitioner (include the name under which you were convicted) Respondent (authorized person having custody of petitioner) PETITIONER V. WARDEN The Attorney General of the State of:	

PETITION

1.
   a. Name and location of court that entered the judgement of conviction you are challenging:

   b. Criminal docket or case number (if you know):

2.
   a. Date of the judgement of conviction

(if you know):

   b. Date of sentencing:
3. Length of sentence:
4. In this case, were you convicted on more than one count or of more than one crime?

ATTACHMENT FIVE

(Example Federal Habeas Motion)

United States District Court Western District of Kentucky
Case Number _____-CV-_____

Petitioner

JOHN DOE	DEFENDENT

VS

WARDEN, JANE DOE	RESPONDENT

MEMORANDUM OF LAW IN SUPPORT OF PETITION FOR WRIT OF HABEAS CORPUS UNDER 28 U.S.C. 2254

STATEMENT OF THE CASE

Around 8:00 p.m. on a July evening, Officer John Doe of the Elizabethtown Police Department was in his vehicle and received a call that people were riding dirt bikes and a four-wheeler in the Walmart parking lot buy the Town Mall.

VR:3/27/17; 1:26:28, 1 :28:44. John immediately proceeded towards that area. Id. at 126:38. When driving towards Walmart, John saw the individuals go through an intersection from Walmart to the Towne Mall area. Id. at 1:27:53. John followed them and executed a traffic stop in the Towne Mall area. Id. Dowell was on the four-wheeler and the other two men were on dirt bikes. Id. at 1:30:25.

NOTES

Chapter 1

[1] <u>Finesse</u>: A mentality that prepares an individual for a fight of some kind.

Chapter 2

[2] <u>Burden of Proof</u>: The false idea that places the onus on the State to prove that you are guilty rather than you having to prove your innocence.

[3] <u>Defendants Mentality</u>: A defendant's disposition of neglecting to disprove one's guilt because of the mistaken belief in the idea of one being innocent until proven guilty.

Chapter 3

[4] <u>5 Felony Weaponry</u>: The 5 most important Constitutional Amendments afforded to those accused of felonies.

[5] <u>Miranda v. Arizona.</u>, 384 U.S. 436

[6] <u>Dismissal w/prejudice</u>: Dismissal of your indictment in a way that the State cannot carry out any future prosecutions against you.

Chapter 4

[7] <u>Caselaw</u>: Appellate Cases through which Judges interpret how

the Constitution applies to various situations and circumstances in a criminal case.

[8] Case-Language: A particular tone a court uses in caselaw when addressing certain matters outside of the issues at hand

[9] Presidential Pyramid: the level of intellectual power each appellate judge holds

Chapter 5
[10] See Attachment #1 for basic outline of a Motion

[11] Pro Se: Self-representation of a defendant

Chapter 6
[12] Pay as You Play: Attorneys that subtly establish a hearing-by-hearing payment arrangement in which you overpay for legal services.

Chapter 7
[13] Faretta v. California., 422 U.S. 806

Chapter 8
[14] Bargaining Power: The degree of doubt the evidence provides prosecutors have that a defendant committed the alleged crime.

[15] E.C.P (Evidentiary Conviction Probability): The degree of likelihood that exists of the evidence against a defendant translating into an actual conviction.

[16] Rules of Evidence: The rules that apply to how evidence is used in criminal cases that each State is governed by.

[17] Inadmissible: A ruling the judge makes declaring that something cannot be introduced during a trial.

[18] Plea Styling: Scrutinizing a plea bargain to determine the degree of interest the prosecution has in prosecuting a defendant.

[19] Conditional Plea: A guilty plea that allows you to further appeal specific and predetermined issues in your case.

[20] Plea agreement: A drawn out plea from prosecution that outlines a plea bargain. You should not confuse a plea agreement with a final judgement.

[21] Final Judgement: A Courts final judgement to the department of corrections as to how your sentence should be served.

Chapter 9

[22] Defense: A particular set of elements that legally correspond to a particular criminal charge in such a way that if proven by a defendant, will avail them at trial.

[23] Ostrich Defense: Elements that entail you had no knowledge of what those around you were going to do.

[24] Derivative Defenses: Elements demonstrating entrapment from law enforcement.

[25] Actus Reus Defenses: Elements which corroborate that the physical act of the alleged crime never occurred.

[26] Jury Instructions: Instructions provided to jury's during

deliberations that outline the all of the necessary basis they must use to utilize their verdict.

Chapter 10

[27] Theory of Facts: The purported facts of how a particular incident took place in criminal proceedings.

[28] Beyond a Reasonable doubt: The standard the jury must use when determining whether a defendant is guilty or innocent.

Chapter 11

[29] Discovery: A record of all of the evidence the prosecution has against you.

Chapter 12

[30] Circumstantial Theory: The manufactured narrative of an alleged crime made to synchronize with the elements of the charge.

[31] Circumstantial Elements: The elements of a criminal offense outlined in jury instructions that inherently impresses the guilt of the defendant.

[32] Presumption: An inductive fact the Court forces the jury to apply to their theory of the case during a trial.

Chapter 13

[33] Narrative Formation: The process of the State controlling a

particular narrative throughout the case.

[34] Bill of Particulars: A request to have the prosecution articulate the most relevant facts of the case.

[35] Presumptive Instructions: An instruction that dictates how jurors are to factor in some manufactured fact when considering jury instructions.

[36] Innocence Oriented Instructions: Jury instructions that frame the facts in such a way that appropriates innocence rather than guilt.

Chapter 14

[37] Initial Probable Cause Hearing: A probable cause hearing to determine if enough probable cause exists to keep you incarcerated.

Chapter 15

[38] Question Instigating: To use one's questions during jury pool to instigate predispositions in jurors.

[39] Jury Socialization: Tactics prosecutors use during voir dire to socially manipulate the jury in trials.

[40] Crossing the Rubicon: A Roman proverb that describes a limit of no return when crossed.

[41] Element Divergence: The subtle and artful use of continuously objecting to a prosecutor questioning of a key witness for purposes of preventing the witness's testimony from weighing

negatively on the elements of the offense.

[42] Reasonable Certainty: A means of enabling a jury to consider both the logic as well as the elements of the prosecution's Circumstantial Theory when determining guilt or innocence.

Chapter 16

[43] Be sure to find out if you occupy one of the few states that do not follow this order.

[44] I.A.C. means ineffective Assistance Counsel

[45] The initials "I.A.C." are used in this book only for the sake of brevity and should never be used in a legal action against a court.

[46] See Bronaugh v. Ohio, 235 F. 3rd 280, 283(6th Cir. 2000)

[47] See Attachment #4 for example of this packet.

[48] Attachment #5 for a basic layout of how you can draft a Federal Habeas Motion

[49] Setting the Record Straight: Preparing the trial record in a way that the appellate court can review your I.A.C. claims on direct appeal.

[50] I.A.A.C.: Ineffective assistance of appellate Counsel, ~a claim that your appellate attorney's representation was ineffective.

[51] Procedural Default: The appellate courts dismiss a defendant's appeal without ever reviewing it, due to the defendant's failure to follow some rule when submitting the appeal.

THE RE-EDUCATION TO TRUE BELIEVING

In his groundbreaking work, Marcus Swan presents an intellectual framework known as Naturalosophy. A philosophical school of thought that possesses the capacity to stimulate the cognitive abilities of individuals who are in pursuit of profound enlightenment. Swan introduces the concept of Naturalosophy and highlights its fundamental aspect, the Re-Education to True Believing.

ISBN 9781-9555-1156

Available at your local bookstores:

        Amazon, Barnes and Nobles and Books A Million

www.ingramcontent.com/pod-product-compliance
Lightning Source LLC
Chambersburg PA
CBHW071303110426
42743CB00042B/1159